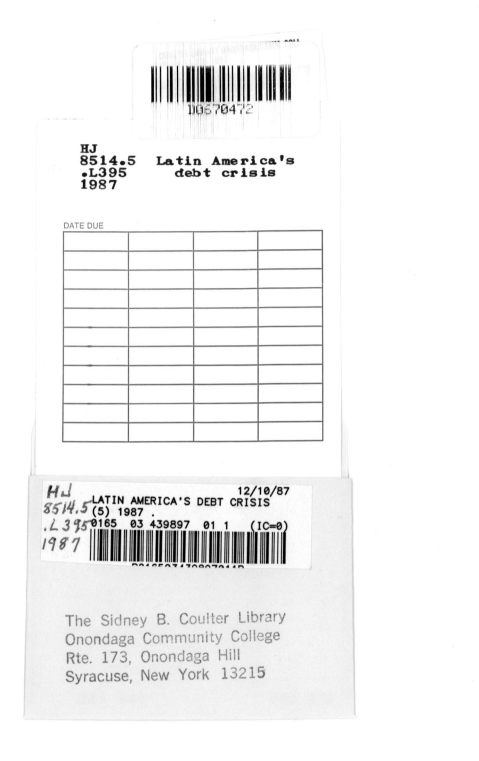

Latin America's Debt Crisis

Latin America's Debt Crisis

Adjusting to the Past or Planning for the Future?

edited by **Robert A. Pastor**

Lynne Rienner Publishers / / Boulder / London

Published in the United States of America in 1987 by
Lynne Rienner Publishers, Inc.
948 North Street, Boulder, Colorado 80302

Library of Congress Cataloging-in-Publication Data

Latin America's debt crisis.

  Bibliography: p.
  Includes index.
  1. Debts, External—Latin America—Congresses.
2. Loans, Foreign—Latin America—Congresses.
I. Pastor, Robert A.
HJ8514.5.L395   1987   336.3'435'098   87-4956
ISBN 1-55587-053-8 (lib. bdg.)

Printed and bound in the United States of America

The paper used in this publication meets the
requirements of the American National Standard
for Permanence of Paper for Printed
Library Materials Z39.48-1984. ⊗

Contents

Tables

Preface

Future students of the Latin American debt crisis of the 1980s may someday wonder why so many talented bankers and finance ministers labored so long and hard to accomplish so little. Since the onset of the debt crisis in 1982, bankers, senior officials from debtor countries, officials from the International Monetary Fund and the World Bank, and officials from the United States and other creditor countries all have negotiated feverishly and almost continuously in search of a formula that would permit the debtor nations to continue paying their debt.

Each formula has failed and has been replaced. Repeated predictions that the crisis was solved have been proven wrong. Latin America's economy—with few exceptions—has continued to deteriorate. However, more serious than the failure to fashion a solution to the debt *as a financial problem* has been the inability to even address the issue *as a development problem*.

During its worst economic depression since the 1930s, Latin America used more than one-third of its foreign exchange each year to service its debt. To pay for its past debt, Latin America has had to mortgage its future development prospects. While trying to adjust to its past, Latin America has found its future opportunities diminished.

This book has three goals. First, the book's contributors try to explain a crisis that preoccupies Latin America but is perceived only dimly in the United States. Second, we assess the costs of the current strategies for dealing with the debt crisis. Finally, the authors offer numerous proposals for addressing debt as a development problem for Latin America and the United States, not just a financial problem for bankers and finance ministers.

This book grew out of a two-day symposium at the Carter Center of Emory University in April 1986. The symposium, convened to address the debt crisis as a long-term issue, assembled a diverse group of experts who are both scholars and policymakers. Their perspectives on the debt crisis range widely. Included in the group were the finance ministers of Venezuela and Mexico, two New York bankers who have played pivotal roles in rescheduling debts, a former president of Costa Rica, a U.S. senator, the western hemisphere director of the International Monetary Fund, a senior Reagan administration official, and several of the best scholars of the debt issue in the world. The participants prepared papers and made presentations, and for two days in April 1986, they debated the issues. This book is the product of their deliberations and their debate, of their consensus and their disagreement. During the symposium, there was wide-ranging discussion moderated by Jimmy Carter and Howard Baker with questions from the audience. We have distilled from that discussion those parts which supplement the chapters and include them in the book.

Since the debt symposium, the papers have been revised numerous times in order to make them as accessible to as wide an audience as possible. Each chapter is brief and to the point. Each offers analysis and prescriptions for what needs to be done.

The debt symposium was the first event sponsored by the Latin American Program of the Carter Center of Emory University. The Carter Center itself was established in 1982 to promote the discussion and development of specific recommendations on topics of contemporary importance through research, public forums, and consultations. In addition to the Latin American program, the Carter Center has projects on the Middle East, arms control, health policy, U.S.-Soviet relations, conflict resolution, and human rights.

The objective of the Latin American program was to raise issues of concern to the United States and Latin America and to seek new ideas and proposals. Former President Jimmy Carter, Rosalynn Carter, and I undertook two extended trips throughout Latin America to discuss ideas for the program with the leaders of the region. The issues that were considered of the greatest importance were the debt crisis, democracy, and Central America. We therefore began our program with a study of long-term development approaches to the debt crisis and then held a major consultation on November 17-18, 1986, on how to reinforce democracy in the Americas.

In each of the conferences, we have sought to approach the central issues in a nonpartisan or a bipartisan manner. The former Majority Leader of the U.S. Senate and current White House Chief of Staff Howard Baker co-chaired the debt symposium with Jimmy Carter, and he not only assured political balance, but also brought a perceptive and informed viewpoint of the debt issue.

The editor of a book such as this has a special obligation to acknowledge his debts. The largest debt is owed to Eric Bord, a young, talented graduate of Emory University, who was indispensable in coordinating the symposium and ensuring that the event was a success. In trying to conceptualize the main questions and themes to be addressed at the symposium, I benefited from the helpful comments of Charles Lipson of the University of Chicago, Albert Fishlow of the University of California, and Jaime Serra Puche, Víctor Urquidi, and Miguel Wionczek of El Colegio de México, where

I taught and examined firsthand the effects of the debt problem in the academic year of 1985/86.

The symposium was co-sponsored by the Institute of the Americas, whose president, Dr. Joseph Grunwald, generously offered his advice and his organization's experience. In addition, the research effort was supported by the Rockefeller Foundation. Betsy Morgan and the Carter Center staff helped organize the symposium. The editorial skills of Faye Goolrick and the word processing abilities of Sheila Carson and Patricia Trotter helped transform the manuscript into a book.

Most of all, the patience and advice of my wife and the vigorous commitment and support of Jimmy and Rosalynn Carter made the symposium and the book possible.

The debt I owe to all of them is more than I can pay.

Robert A. Pastor

Latin America's Debt and U.S. Interests

Jimmy Carter and Howard Baker

Jimmy Carter

Today, Latin America is faced with many problems, but none is as serious as the debt crisis. This conclusion is widely shared throughout Latin America, as I found on three separate trips there from 1984 to 1986. During these trips, I held discussions with the presidents and other leaders of Brazil, Argentina, Peru, Venezuela, Colombia, Panama, Costa Rica, Nicaragua, El Salvador, and Mexico.

In every one of these countries, with the partial exceptions of Nicaragua and El Salvador, our discussions were drawn to the debt crisis. For Latin Americans, the debt crisis has obstructed their strong desire for economic progress, human rights, and social justice. In my conversation with President Jaime Lusinchi of Venezuela, to take one example, he described his goal of expanding nonpetroleum exports, but then explained that his government does not have the capital to achieve this objective because of the burden of servicing the debt.

In Costa Rica, in February 1986, I met with Luis Alberto Monge, who completed his term as president three months later, and then I met with his successor, Oscar Arias. The United States has been providing about $130 million of foreign aid to Costa Rica each year, but little of that money leaves the United States. It goes from the government in Washington to the banks in New York to pay the interest on Costa Rica's debt. U.S. taxpayers might think that they are helping to improve the quality of life for the people of Costa Rica—one of the sterling democracies in the world—but ironically, much of the aid money is used to service that nation's external debt.

Latin America's obsession with the debt crisis is not misplaced, but it is not shared by the United States. Many in this country view the crisis as a distant problem and do not want to assume any responsibility for it. The U.S. population hopes the debt crisis will go away, but it will not go away, and it will not get better unless the United States is more helpful than it has been so far.

The United States has both an economic and an idealistic interest in resolving the debt crisis. Because Latin America needs to use so many of the dollars it earns to pay the interest on its debt, it has had to reduce its purchases of U.S. goods. In the four-year period from 1981 to 1984, the U.S. trade balance was hurt more by the decline in *exports to Latin America* than by the increase in *imports from Japan*. Estimates range from 400,000 to 1 million U.S. jobs lost as a result of the declining exports to Latin America.

The United States also is crucially interested in the vitality of democracies in the hemisphere. External debt has become a serious destabilizing factor. Some countries have to use one-third to one-half their total export earnings to service their foreign debt. Governments therefore do not have the funds to invest in education, health, or development, and inevitably, some people will ask whether democracy is an improvement over dictatorship.

The United States shares fundamental economic and humanitarian interests with Latin America in trying to solve the debt crisis. This book offers some specific solutions that the people of the Americas should consider seriously to address this crisis—and to forge a true partnership of the Americas.

Howard Baker

In this book, the authors assess the economic, political, and social costs of the debt crisis for Latin America, but they also present the costs of the current solutions. Most debtor countries have applied the conventional solutions of restructuring and rescheduling their debt while at the same time attempting to adjust their macroeconomic policies through austerity to generate trade surpluses. It may be that the current cure—austerity and high debt service— is killing the patient.

The chapters in the first part of the book address the question of the costs of the current solutions—the economic, social, political, and environmental costs to Latin America. But the costs to the United States also are great. Of course, the major U.S. banks are very concerned, because of their exposure, but the United States has other equally substantial economic interests in terms of trade and investment with Latin America. The United States also has a significant strategic interest in Latin America. North Americans are concerned about regional stability and the preservation and enhancement of democratic institutions, which now are flourishing throughout most of the region.

This book, therefore, is significant because it moves the discussion about the debt crisis from the technical/economic arena so often dominated by the banks to the political arena where the banks' interests, although still critical, are viewed from a political and strategic perspective. The book also underscores the renewed commitment of the U.S. government to seek a long-term and workable solution to the debt crisis.

The unveiling of the Baker (James A. Baker III) Plan in the fall of 1985 was a major initiative by the Reagan administration to move the crisis to a higher political level. Because the plan of Secretary of the Treasury Baker encourages the World Bank to play a larger role, the Reagan administration, in my view, showed remarkable wisdom in appointing former Congressman Barber Conable, a widely respected politician, to be president of the World Bank.

The economic, political, and social aspects of the debt crisis result in a complex matrix. No solution will be easy, and no solution, whether short term or long term, conventional or radical, will be without its costs. In fact, I believe that radical unilateral solutions will prove to be prohibitively costly, probably unaffordable, and almost surely not the real solution to the complex problem that confronts the western hemisphere.

It is therefore in everyone's interest to work out a long-term, mutually acceptable solution. In the decades to come, I hope that the people of both North America and South America, men and women throughout this hemisphere, will be able to look back with admiration on our wisdom, our policies, and the directed movement of our efforts at this time. I hope, as well, that they understand the enormous patience and commitment required to solve these problems.

chapter one

The Debt Crisis: A Financial or a Development Problem?

Robert A. Pastor

In an address to the United Nations on September 23, 1985, President Alan García of Peru tried to awaken the conscience of the international community to an insidious dilemma. "We are faced," he said, "with a dramatic choice: It is either debt or democracy."[1]

Although the choices today are not as stark as they were painted by President García, they soon may be. One of the reasons for the resurgence of democracy in the late 1970s and 1980s was that the military could not cope with the consequences of expanding debts. Whether the new civilian democratic governments can cope with the debt crisis any more effectively remains to be seen. Much will depend on the response by the international community, which includes the commercial banks, the International Monetary Fund (IMF) and the World Bank, and the debtor and creditor governments.

Thus far, the international community has done the minimal necessary to reduce the threat to the international financial system. The debt has been defined as a financial—or a liquidity—problem, and the international community has devised a strategy that has succeeded in avoiding defaults. Debtor nations have had to accept a rigorous package of austerity policies in order to obtain loans from the IMF and private banks. In addition, the debtor nations and the banks have rescheduled the debt to postpone principal payments, reduce commissions or fees, and extend the maturities and the grace periods of the short-term debt.

If one defines the crisis in financial terms and sees the stability of the international financial system at risk, then one might view the response as successful because the international financial system has not collapsed. However, although the stability of the international financial system is an important—perhaps the most important—criterion for judging debt policies, it is hardly the only one. Other important criteria include political stability and the economic development of Latin America, other debtor regions, and the United States as well. Moreover, one needs to ask whether a particular strategy is the correct one if it postpones an outcome that may be made worse because it is repeatedly postponed. The question, in brief, is whether we have been saving time or losing it.

"You can see a lot just by looking," Yogi Berra once said. "Just by looking" the sensitive eye could see the debris of the debt crisis throughout Latin America. The unrepaired roads, the watersystem that feeds only half a city, the increased cases of malnutrition and of infant deaths, the construction that has stopped—these are all illustrations of development that has been halted while scarce resources are sent abroad to pay the debt.[2]

Statistics are not as moving as images, but they do help one to decide which anecdotes are illustrative and which are misleading. By 1985, the per capita product of Latin America was 9 percent less than that of 1980, or roughly the level that the region had achieved in 1977. Latin America had lost a decade of development, and only the most optimistic scenarios suggest that by 1990 the region will attain the level it had reached a decade before. Latin America will remember that its debt burden precipitated and exacerbated its worst economic crisis since the Great Depression.[3]

One characteristic, it was thought, of a developing nation is that it imports capital to promote its development. The United States, for example, was a major capital importer in the nineteenth century. From 1960 to about 1980, Latin America received billions of dollars from the United States and Europe, and that investment helped fuel one of the most dynamic development experiences in the world. From 1973 to 1981, Latin America received a net transfer of $91.8 billion from abroad. The gross domestic product (GDP) of Latin America during this period tripled, and per capita income increased at an average annual rate of 3.3 percent.

For a number of reasons, including high interest rates and the oil price shock, the debt accumulated very rapidly at the end of the 1970s. As a result, Latin America suddenly began sending dollars abroad rather than receiving them. During just four years, from 1982 to 1985, the net transfer of capital from Latin America amounted to $106.7 billion—more than the region had received during the previous nine years.[4] Latin America had been transformed into a region that was exporting capital to richer countries on a massive scale. Even discounting for inflation, Latin America transferred more to richer countries in those four years than the United States transferred to Latin America during the decade of the Alliance for Progress.

These flows did not include "capital flight," money sent by Latin Americans into foreign bank accounts. The U.S. State Department has estimated capital flight at more than $100 billion since 1980.[5] If one adds the private capital flight together with the public debt service, Latin America has transferred more than $200 billion to the United States and other industrialized countries since 1980. This amounts to more than twelve times the Marshall Plan in current dollars.

The debt became a drag on Latin America's quest for development. Capital was diverted from domestic investment to international debt service. Instead of investing in its future, the region had to pay for its past spending. Instead of planning for its development, the region's leaders were impelled to adjust the economies and the lives of the people to a continually declining standard of living.

The authors of this book address two sets of questions. What are the costs of the current strategy to deal with the debt crisis? Can the international community fashion a plan that would permit Latin America to reduce its debt burden and invest in its future again?

The Origin and the Magnitude of the Debt Crisis

The debt crisis originated in a fundamental shift in the supply and demand for money. In the 1970s, as a result of two "oil shocks," the oil-producing nations of the world found themselves with more money than they could consume or invest. They transferred most of the money to private banks, which in turn recycled the money, mostly to the advanced developing nations.

The demand for dollars in those nations had surged for other reasons. Many of these nations already had begun to borrow on the international capital markets to finance fiscal and balance-of-payments deficits. At the same time, independent of the governments, state-owned enterprises accumulated massive deficits and external debts.[6]

While Latin America turned to the commercial banks for financing, the multilateral development banks were shifting much of their concessional lending toward poorer nations, and foreign direct investment in Latin America also declined in relative importance. The cumulative effect was a change in the composition and nature of Latin America's debt—from official, concessional, and long term to private, shorter term, and with higher interest rates. In 1961, more than 50 percent of Latin America's external debt was owed to official sources; that diminished to 36 percent by 1970 and 12 percent by 1982.[7]

The banks had more capital to lend, and the advanced developing nations—particularly the oil-importing nations—found themselves more in need of capital. When the second "oil shock" occurred in the years 1979 and 1980, the U.S. Federal Reserve Bank reacted to the inflationary effect of the increased oil prices with a stringent monetary policy that increased short-term interest rates in the United States from 8.2 percent in 1978 to 15.9 percent in 1981.[8] The effect on the borrowing developing nations was catastrophic, but few realized it until it was too late.

The external debt of all developing countries increased from less than $400 billion in 1978 to about $900 billion in 1985.[9] Latin America not only holds the largest portion of the debt of all developing countries, but it also has had the most rapid increase. While the debt of the developing world increased nearly eleven times since 1970, Latin America's debt increased sixteenfold (see Table 1.1). From 1978 to 1982, Latin America's external debt increased from $151 billion to $318 billion, and the percentage of that debt owed to commercial banks rose to 88 percent. By the end of 1986, Latin America's total disbursed external debt was $382 billion.

Within Latin America, Brazil, Mexico, Argentina, and Venezuela account for three-quarters of the debt. Of the $303 billion of private debt, about 40 percent is owed to U.S. banks, of which nine banks account for 62 percent of that total (Bank of America, Citibank, Chemical, Chase Manhattan, Morgan Guaranty Trust Company, Manufacturers Hanover, Continental Illinois, Bankers Trust, and First National Bank of Chicago). In short, Latin America has the lion's share of the debt in the developing world, and that debt is concentrated in four countries.

The burden, of course, is not so much the debt, but the annual debt service payments. No clearer example of the onset of the debt crisis can be

Table 1.1 Latin America and the Caribbean: External Debt, 1970-1985

	Total Debt	Debt from Official Sources		Debt from Private Sources	
	Billions of Dollars	Billions of Dollars	As a % of the Total Debt	Billions of Dollars	As a % of the Total Debt
1970	23	8	36	15	64
1971	26	9	36	17	64
1972	30	10	34	20	66
1973	40	12	28	28	72
1974	56	14	25	42	75
1975	75	16	22	59	78
1976	98	18	18	80	82
1977	116	21	18	95	82
1978	151	25	16	127	84
1979	182	27	15	157	85
1980	223	31	14	198	86
1981	278	34	12	246	88
1982	318	40	12	278	88
1983	344	51	15	293	85
1984	360	57	16	303	84
1985	368	65	18	303	82

Source: U.N. Economic Commission for Latin America and the Caribbean, *The Problem of the External Debt: Gestation, Development, Crisis, and Prospects,* March 6, 1986, Table 4, 8.

seen than the explosion of interest payments from 15.7 percent of export earnings in 1978 to 41 percent in 1982 (see Table 1.2). Since then, interest payments have remained more than one-third of exports—a debilitating, high ratio.

The severity of the crisis was partly the result of mistaken macroeconomic policies. In the 1970s, many developing nations—particularly the oil-exporting nations such as Mexico and Venezuela—maintained overvalued exchange rates, which discouraged non-oil exports and encouraged many citizens to invest abroad and in foreign currencies. "Capital flight" was a problem before the debt crisis, but it became much more acute as a result of the crisis.

The Evolution of the Crisis: Three Phases

While banks and debtor nations have negotiated many rounds of reschedulings, the debt crisis has evolved through three distinct phases: (1) The Bubble Bursts, August 1982–November 1983; (2) The Merry-Go-Round of Reschedulings, November 1983–February 1986; and (3) The Relentless Crisis, February 1986–present. Each phase represented a realization that the crisis was not solved, indeed, that it had worsened, and that it required a more elaborate response.

The Bubble Bursts

Most analysts date the beginning of the modern debt crisis to the announcement by the Mexican Minister of Finance Jésus Silva-Herzog in August 1982 that his government could no longer service its debt.[10] The United States responded quickly by assembling an emergency package of credits that permitted Mexico to maintain its obligations while negotiating a standby agreement with the IMF. Mexico then negotiated a restructuring of its debt, and the banks agreed to increase their total exposure in Mexico by 7 percent. This was known as the "7 percent solution" and the beginning of "involuntary lending" by the banks.[11]

If the debt problem had stopped with Mexico, it would not have been a crisis. However, the problem *started* with Mexico. Fearful that they had already overextended themselves, the private banks reduced or ceased their loans to most of Latin America, thus exacerbating the crisis. Other Latin American governments, in similar difficulties, demanded debt reschedulings. The International Monetary Fund stepped into the breach and prevented the debt crisis from precipitating a collapse of the international financial system.

Table 1.2   Latin America and the Caribbean: Ratio of Total Interest Payments to Exports of Goods and Services, 1978-1986 (percentages)

Country	1978	1979	1980	1981	1982	1983	1984	1985	1986
Latin America	15.7	17.6	20.2	28.0	41.0	36.0	35.6	35.2	35.1
Oil-exporting countries	**16.1**	**15.7**	**16.6**	**22.6**	**35.6**	**31.4**	**32.5**	**32.3**	**36.5**
Bolivia	13.7	18.6	25.0	34.5	43.4	39.8	49.8	46.8	46.7
Ecuador	10.4	13.6	18.3	24.3	30.0	27.4	30.7	27.0	32.2
Mexico	24.0	24.5	23.3	29.0	47.3	37.5	39.0	36.0	40.0
Peru	21.2	15.5	16.0	24.1	25.1	29.8	33.2	30.0	27.3
Venezuela	7.2	6.9	8.1	12.7	21.0	21.6	20.1	26.3	33.3
Non-oil-exporting countries	**15.5**	**19.3**	**23.7**	**33.6**	**46.7**	**40.7**	**38.7**	**37.9**	**34.2**
Argentina	9.6	12.8	22.0	35.5	53.6	58.4	57.6	51.1	51.8
Brazil	24.5	31.5	34.1	40.4	57.1	43.5	39.7	40.0	37.7
Colombia	7.5	9.9	11.8	21.9	25.9	26.7	22.8	26.3	18.6
Costa Rica	9.9	12.8	18.0	28.0	36.1	33.0	26.6	27.3	22.7
Chile	16.9	16.5	19.3	38.8	49.5	38.9	48.0	43.5	39.2
Dominican Republic	14.0	14.3	14.8	19.1	22.7	24.5	18.1	22.2	27.1
El Salvador	5.3	5.7	5.9	7.8	11.9	12.2	12.3	12.6	10.3
Guatemala	3.7	3.2	5.3	7.6	7.8	8.7	12.3	14.9	14.9
Haiti	2.8	3.2	2.1	2.7	2.4	2.4	5.3	4.2	5.7
Honduras	8.2	8.6	10.6	14.4	22.4	16.4	15.8	15.3	12.7
Nicaragua	9.3	9.7	17.8	21.9	32.1	14.3	12.1	13.0	25.8
Paraguay	8.4	10.7	13.4	14.8	13.5	14.3	10.1	8.3	10.1
Uruguay	10.4	9.0	11.0	12.9	22.4	24.8	34.8	34.2	23.8

Source: U.N. Economic Commission for Latin America and the Caribbean, *Economic Survey of Latin America and the Caribbean, 1986,* Table 16, 22.

The IMF applied a standard formula to each case. It would orchestrate the negotiations for a financial package that would include debt rescheduling and new loans in exchange for an agreement by the debtor nation to modify its macroeconomic policies, adopt a more realistic exchange rate, and reduce its fiscal deficit.

The first phase of the debt crisis can be said to have ended in November 1983 with two events. First, after months of negotiations, Brazil finally accepted a package of austerity measures in exchange for IMF credits and new loans. Second, the U.S. Congress approved an $8.4 billion appropriation to fund an enlarged IMF quota and an expansion of the IMF's General Arrangements to Borrow. U.S. support was important not only because the IMF's resources were dangerously low, but also because it signaled the beginning of a positive change in the Reagan administration's view of the international financial institutions.

The Merry-Go-Round of Reschedulings

Some considered the debt crisis as virtually over. According to this view, the international economy would begin to grow, and industrialized nations would accept increasing exports from the debtor nations. As this occurred, the crisis would diminish and perhaps end. A few argued that the rescheduling packages were mere palliatives and would not solve the problem.[12] Both views had some validity. In 1984, the world economy grew, and the U.S. economy in particular expanded sufficiently to purchase 85 percent of the increased exports from Latin America. Still, the problem hardly was solved.

The austerity policies were technically successful in reducing fiscal deficits and cutting imports, but Latin America as a whole had to transfer abroad more than one-third of its export earnings each year to pay its debt. That debt did not shrink either in absolute terms or as a percentage of exports or GDP, despite the severe adjustment. Argentina, Brazil, Mexico, and Peru were among the larger countries that found the previous arrangements unworkable and sought new reschedulings (see Table 1.3). Debt renegotiations continued almost without stop.

As weary of the annual reschedulings as their counterparts, bankers began negotiating multiyear rescheduling arrangements. This not only allowed the finance ministers to work on something other than the debt, but it also reintroduced some stability to their economic planning.

In this second phase, the World Bank began to play a larger role, joining the IMF in developing loan programs that would permit a longer-term adjustment of the affected economies. But commercial bank funds were scarce and the debt burden so severe that debt reschedulings increased in number and amount in 1985; a total of twelve agreements were negotiated for a total amount of $87 billion. In this second phase, average surcharges on the reference rate charged by the banks were reduced from about 2.22 percent greater than the London interbank offered rated (LIBOR) to 1.77 percent, while the commissions charged by the banks declined from about 1.2 percent to about 0.8 percent.[13] However, the benefits of longer-term debt, reduced commissions, and lower market interest rates were offset by the continuing decline in the terms of trade.

By September 1985, it was increasingly clear that the old formula was not working. Brazil, Mexico, and Argentina—the big three—were unable to stay within the parameters of IMF agreements, and Alan García had thrown down a new challenge to the banks at his inauguration in July 1985. García linked the payment of interest with export earnings and declared that Peru would not pay more than 10 percent annually. He also tried to organize his fellow presidents to support and adopt his proposal.

Table 1.3   Latin America and the Caribbean: Rescheduling of External Debt with Private Banks, 1982-1985 (millions of dollars)

	First Round 1982-1983			Second Round 1983-1984			Third Round 1984-1985		
	Maturities		New Credits	Maturities		New Credits	Maturities		New Credits
	Amount	Years	Amount	Amount	Years	Amount	Amount	Years	Amount
Argentina	13,000	Sep. 82-83	1,500	-	-	-	13,500	82-85	4,200
Brazil	4,800	83	4,400	5,400	84	6,500	-	-	-
Costa Rica	650	82-84	225	-	-	-	280	85-86	75
Chile	3,424	83-84	1,300	-	-	780	5,932	85-87	714 371
Cuba	130	Sep. 82-83	-	103	84	-	82	85	-
Dominican Republic	568	82-83	-	-	-	-	790	82-85	-
Ecuador	1,970	Nov. 82-83	431	900	84	-	4,630	85-89	200
Honduras	121	82-84	-	-	-	-	220	85-86	-
Mexico	23,700	Aug. 82-84	5,000	12,000	Aug. 82-84	3,800	48,700	85-90	-
Panama	180	83	100	-	-	-	603	85-86	60
Peru	400	83	450	662	84- Jul. 85	-	-	-	-
Uruguay	630	83-84	240	-	-	-	1,600	85-89	-
Venezuela	-	-	-	-	-	-	21,200	83-88	-

Source: U.N. Economic Commission for Latin American and the Caribbean, *Economic Survey of Latin America and the Caribbean, 1985,* Table 18, 33.

New money and attention were necessary. As it appeared that Latin America might adopt a unified approach to the problem, U.S. Secretary of the Treasury James A. Baker seized the initiative. Previously, the United States had remained in the background on the debt issue, but Baker offered a plan at the IMF/World Bank annual meeting in October 1985 in Seoul, South Korea. That plan called for an increase of $9 billion in official lending during a three-year period, an increase of $20 billion in bank loans, and a less statist, more export-oriented development strategy by the debtor nations. The private banks promised to be helpful.

The group of Latin American debtor nations—known as the Cartagena Group, named for the site of their first meeting on June 22, 1984—met in Montevideo in December 1985 to assess the Baker Plan. The group agreed that Secretary Baker's proposal was a positive step but was inadequate to meet their needs. The group also made a specific set of proposals. It recommended (1) a sharp decline in real interest rates; (2) concessional terms on old debts and market terms for new loans; (3) an increase in bank lending; and (4) a linkage between the amount a country pays in interest and other debt services with its minimum economic growth targets.[14]

This last point stemmed from a set of recommendations that had emerged from a meeting of Latin American economists in Oaxtepec, Mexico, in July 1985 that had insisted that growth was the only way to exit the debt crisis. If Latin America could grow, it could pay the debt. But Latin America could not grow if it kept exporting so much capital. The Oaxtepec group decided to reverse the formula for approaching the debt crisis. Instead of sacrificing growth to debt service, the group decided to set the growth targets first, and whatever debt service could be managed within those targets would be paid.[15]

The Relentlessness of the Debt Crisis

While governments, banks, and international institutions sought ways to adapt the standard IMF formula to new realities and concepts such as "grow to pay," a second "Mexican crisis" altered the terms of the debate. Mexico had fallen out of compliance with the IMF in September 1985, days before two earthquakes shook the country. Before Mexico could identify where it would locate the extra foreign exchange needed for reconstruction, it was hammered by an even worse economic shock. The price of oil plummeted from $30.80 (for one barrel of West Texas intermediate crude) on November 21, 1985, to $11.50 on April 2, 1986—a decline of 64 percent. Oil and gas exports accounted for about 70 percent of Mexico's foreign exchange in 1984, or roughly $16.6 billion. With the collapse in the price, Mexico estimated that it would lose about $7 billion in oil revenues in 1986.

Having failed to make much progress in adapting the Baker Plan to their needs, several Latin American governments apparently decided to let Mexico run interference for them. The United States, they thought, was more likely to assist Mexico because of its strategic importance. Therefore, several decided to await the outcome of those negotiations and use that as a precedent.

Mexico reached an agreement with the IMF in July 1986 and with its commercial bank creditors on September 30. Although the Mexican government initially had sought some form of debt relief, and while public opinion in Mexico began to coalesce around the need for a debt moratorium, the long negotiations yielded additional loans totaling $12.5 billion—half from the international development banks and half from the private banks. There were some new facets to this agreement, including an additional $1.7 billion in loans to be activated in the event of an unanticipated deterioration in the

Mexican economy. In addition, more than five hundred banks agreed to restructure $43.7 billion in old debt during a twenty-year period with a seven-year grace period and at reduced interest rates.[16]

The Mexican agreement was not the precedent originally envisaged.[17] It was, in effect, another postponement of a difficult problem—an accumulation of new debt rather than a reduction of the old debt.

In 1986, most Latin American governments found themselves once again renegotiating their debts. Venezuela signed an agreement in February but had to renegotiate it by the end of the year because of the drop in oil prices. Argentina, Brazil, Ecuador, and many other governments were compelled to seek new credits with the private banks and new arrangements with the IMF.

The clearest sign, however, that the debt crisis was continuing to frustrate the hopes and prospects of Latin America occurred on February 20, 1987, when the president of Brazil José Sarney announced a unilateral suspension of interest payments to foreign commercial banks. One year before, many bankers and economists, who were expressing dismay with Mexico's economic problems, looked to Brazil's spectacular economic performance to reassure themselves that the debt crisis was manageable. Therefore, when Brazil suspended payments on $81 billion of private debt (a total of $108 billion), it stunned the international banking community.

Three weeks later on March 13, after earthquakes killed hundreds of people and broke the country's main oil pipeline, Ecuador's president also suspended payments on its $8.3 billion debt. Bolivia also could not make payments on its debt, and the question was whether other governments would follow with unilateral decisions to suspend payments.

The Brazilian finance minister noted that Brazil paid $45 billion in interest and received only $11 billion in new credits since 1983. "[The situation has] to be changed so that debtor countries can continue to grow and participate in markets and trade and can service their debts through development and not recession."[18] This view remains widely shared in Latin America: the governments do not want to opt out of the international economy; they want to participate as partners. To do so, however, requires writing down the debt. Unfortunately, there still seems little evidence of the kind of political will in the industrialized world necessary to exit the debt crisis.

The Costs of Current "Solutions"

While some have called for a solution to the debt crisis, others suggest it cannot be solved, only alleviated. But the international community has fashioned a "solution" whose principal aim is to permit the Latin American debtor nations to continue paying their debts. The austerity policies that Latin America has had to accept in order to obtain new funds have created unemployment, reduced domestic investment, and contributed to a diminution of the standard of living of the region's people.

The overarching question is whether the benefits of this solution exceed the costs. In the first part of this book, a number of authors examine this question. Terence Canavan examines the costs to the international banks. It is worth noting that the U.S. banking system also has suffered severe shocks, not just because of flawed loans to Latin America but also because of serious financial problems in the U.S. oil and farming industries.[19]

In a unique contribution to understanding a concealed dimension of the debt issue, Gustave Speth identifies the costs to natural resources and the environment and also recommends a number of policies to transform the challenge of the environment into an opportunity. Daniel Oduber, a former president of Costa Rica, describes the social and political impact of the debt crisis. The new democracies in the region are all the more vulnerable because they have remitted funds to the industrialized countries rather than investing those same funds at home. Finally, Jésus Silva-Herzog, the former minister of finance of Mexico, analyzes the heavy economic costs borne by Latin America. Indeed, Silva-Herzog, who was forced to resign in June 1986, was himself a casualty of the third phase of the debt crisis.

Senator Bill Bradley describes the costs of the debt crisis to the United States. By 1985, Latin America, which purchases about one-third of its imports from the United States, was forced to reduce imports to $63 billion, down from more than $100 billion in 1981. This loss in exports means a significant loss in U.S. jobs.

Although the costs of the debt crisis are the more obvious, some have noted that it also has had salutary effects. As the western hemisphere director of the International Monetary Fund, Eduardo Wiesner is acutely aware of the principal benefit of the current solution to the debt crisis—the international financial system, which was endangered by the debt overhang, has been maintained. But Wiesner also notes a number of other positive effects. Exchange rates are now more realistic; Argentina, for example, devalued its peso by 50 percent in 1985/86. Fiscal deficits as a percentage of gross domestic product have plummeted by 50 percent in many countries. Trade deficits were replaced by significant surpluses. In comparison, and not without a trace of irony, the United States has been unable to take any steps that could match Latin America in trimming either its fiscal or trade deficit. Indeed, in 1986, the United States became the world's largest debtor nation, surpassing Brazil and Mexico.

After assessing the benefits and the costs, the reader can draw his or her own conclusions about the net gain or loss of the current solution to the debt crisis.

Debt Crises of the Past and Present

The second half of this book is devoted to analyzing and developing new ideas and proposals to deal with the current debt crisis. To better understand the feasibility of new proposals, it would be useful to step back and examine how previous debt crises have been resolved. By identifying both the similarities and the differences from previous experiences, one can better judge the opportunities as well as the limitations of new proposals.

The first debt crisis occurred soon after Latin America achieved independence in the 1820s. The new Latin American governments contracted large loans with European, mostly English, bankers. Virtually all of these loans "went into swift default."[20] The Latin American governments stopped payments of interest and principal, and there were no rollovers or reschedulings. Needless to say, there were no more loans either—at least for about forty years.

The memory of this default lasted until the next economic boom in Europe in the 1860s. Once again, the Europeans, led by the British, began lending money to Latin American governments and also making direct investments in the region. Because of periodic depressions and political instability, more than one-half of all the bonds were in default by the 1880s. Given that two-thirds of all British investment in Latin America was in government bonds, the defaults obviously affected both the flow of capital to the region and British policy.

The British government decided, however, that "it was cheaper to bear the immediate costs of occasional bond defaults than to risk sabotaging local governments by frequent interventions." The British were hardly passive— they threatened or used force to try to compel payments in Latin America forty times from 1820 to 1914—but by the standards of the day, they were relatively restrained.[21] However, by 1914, a large part of Latin America's debt was in default, and new funding stopped for that reason and also because of the war.[22]

During World War I, many Europeans disinvested, and after the war, Europe had its own debt problem. Germany was obligated to pay $30 billion of war reparations to the Allies in Europe, which, in turn, owed the United States $20 billion. The war left Europe devastated, but the Allies would not relieve Germany of its debt without some relief from the United States. President Coolidge would not hear of it, but in 1924, the United States did negotiate the Dawes Plan, which resulted in the United States loaning new money to Germany to pay the Allies, which would then pay the United States.

This plan broke down in 1929 when the United States could no longer loan money to Germany. The new Young Plan reduced the German debt by 20 percent and stretched it to fifty years, but the world depression soon made any payments impossible. Germany stopped paying in 1931, and President Hoover declared a moratorium.

Loans to Latin America fared no better. In the 1920s, U.S. investors gradually replaced the Europeans in Latin America. Secretary of Commerce Herbert Hoover warned U.S. investment bankers to be more cautious about floating bonds in Latin America, but they did not listen. Hoover was concerned about both the volume of bonds and the precariousness of the particular investments. Hoover did not believe that the U. S. government ought to intervene in order to protect such investors; he tried to discourage risky investments in order to minimize the possibility of default that could provoke U.S. intervention.[23]

The stock market crash in 1929 precipitated and exacerbated the world depression. It was widely known that Latin American, German, and Allied debts would not be repaid, but no officials would say so publicly. Instead, the United States drafted new plans that would permit payments to continue, but the severity of the economic crisis made that impossible.

In December 1930, Bolivia defaulted. Peru followed three months later and Chile four months after that. In September 1931, Brazil defaulted, and by the end of 1933, all the Latin American countries except Argentina and Haiti had undertaken unilateral moratoriums; they stopped paying their debts.[24]

The only novel proposal to emerge from the 1930s debt crisis was an offer by President Herbert Hoover to cancel the debt of the British government in exchange for Bermuda, British Honduras, and Trinidad. The British rejected the offer.[25]

After World War II, the United States and Great Britain established two international organizations to regulate international finance and assistance for reconstruction and development: the IMF and the World Bank. The World Bank insisted that before making a loan, the receiving government would have to reach a satisfactory settlement on bonds that it had previously defaulted, including some that were issued in the nineteenth century. In all cases, such settlements were reached, sometimes at great discounts.[26] Mexico, for example, settled its outstanding debt at the rate of one peso per dollar.[27] In looking back, one Mexican scholar drew the following conclusion: "Most of the bonds issued in the nineteenth and early twentieth centuries to developing countries, even those secured by government guarantee, have either never been amortized or have become worthless on the market, fit only to be used as wallpaper."[28]

What are the similarities and differences between the debt crisis of the 1930s and that of the 1980s? Both coincided with global depressions, although the former was much more serious, widespread, and lasted longer. In both periods, Latin America owed the United States more money than it

8. International Monetary Fund, *World Economic Outlook* (Washington, D.C.: IMF, April 1986), Table A15, p. 194.

9. Ibid., Table A47, p. 243.

10. For a detailed case study of the events during this crisis, see Joseph Kraft, *The Mexican Rescue* (New York: Group of Thirty, 1984).

11. Charles F. Meissner, "Crisis as an Opportunity for Change: A Commentary on the Debt Restructuring Process," *Journal of International Law and Politics* 17, no. 3 (Spring 1985): pp. 619–620.

12. Albert Fishlow was one of the few who wrote that the crisis was not over. See his "The Debt Crisis: Round Two Ahead?" in Richard E. Feinberg (ed.), *Adjustment Crisis in the Third World* (New Brunswick, N.J.: Transaction, 1984).

13. U.N. Economic Commission for Latin America and the Caribbean, *Latin American and Caribbean Development: Obstacles, Requirements and Options,* November 25, 1986, p. 141, n. 74.

14. S. Karen Witcher, "Latin American Debtors Display an Unusual Degree of Agreement," *Wall Street Journal,* December 23, 1985.

15. Comunicado de Oaxtepec, "Eficiencia en el Manejo de la Deuda Externa en América Latina" (Efficiency in the Management of the External Debt in Latin America), Oaxtepec, Mexico, July 1985. I am grateful to Jaime Serra for bringing the results of that conference to my attention.

16. Eric N. Berg, "Agreement on Loan to Mexico," *New York Times,* October 1, 1986, pp. 29, 36.

17. Eric N. Berg, "Mexico Debt Link Seen as Precedent," *New York Times,* October 2, 1986, pp. 25, 28.

18. Alan Riding, "Brazil Talking to Nations, Not Banks, on Debt," *New York Times,* February 27, 1987, p. 38.

19. In *The New York Times,* see two articles by Nathaniel C. Nash, "Washington Watch: Bank Failure Costs Rising," January 12, 1987, p. 27; and "FDIC Chief Sees Bank Failure Rise," January 22, 1987. The administration estimated that bank failures in 1987 would cost taxpayers about $10 billion. In the early 1980s, an average of 10 banks failed every year in the United States. In 1986, a record 145 banks failed, and the chairman of the Federal Deposit Insurance Corporation, William Seidman, predicted that the number of failures could rise by as much as 25 percent in 1987.

20. Charles Lipson, *Standing Guard: Protecting Foreign Capital in the Nineteenth and Twentieth Centuries* (Berkeley: University of California Press, 1985), p. 43.

21. Ibid., pp. 45, 54.

22. Víctor L. Urquidi, "The Long-Term Consequences of the Global Debt Problem" (Paper prepared for the International Federation of Institutes for Advanced Study, Solna, Sweden, 1985), p. 3.

23. Joan Hoff Wilson, *American Business and Foreign Policy* (Boston: Beacon Press, 1971), Chapter 4.

24. Ibid., pp. 133, 178. Haiti did not default because the United States already had a customs receivership.

25. Ibid., p. 128.

26. Edward S. Mason and Robert E. Asher, *The World Bank Since Bretton Woods* (Washington, D.C.: Brookings Institution, 1973), pp. 155–163, 336–339.

27. Víctor L. Urquidi, "The Long-Term Consequences of the Global Debt Problem," p. 4.

28. Ibid., p. 17.

part one

The Magnitude of the Problem and the Costs of Current Solutions

chapter two

The State of the Debt Crisis: Benefits and Costs

Eduardo Wiesner

To provide some perspective on the debt crisis, I first present a brief summary of the progress that has been achieved since 1982. Then, I address the current problem and some of the key policy requirements needed for sustained growth, and last, I review some of the main features of the Baker Initiative.

Developments and Progress to Date

One can identify four major areas where progress has been achieved since 1982: in fiscal adjustment, external adjustment, global economic conditions, and international cooperation. Fiscal deficits, which were the most important factor behind the insurgence of the debt crisis, have been reduced substantially in a good number of countries. Between 1982 and 1984, Argentina, Brazil, Mexico, Venezuela, Ecuador, Costa Rica, and Uruguay more than halved their nonfinancial public sector deficits as a percentage of gross domestic product.

As for external adjustment, the strengthening of the fiscal position in these countries and in others contributed to a very substantial improvement in the current account of the balance of payments of the region. For Latin America as a whole, the current account deficit was reduced from an average of $43 billion a year in 1981 and 1982 to less than $10 billion a year in 1984 and 1985. The three largest countries—Argentina, Brazil, and Mexico—reduced their combined current account deficit from $29.6 billion in 1981 to $3.5 billion in 1983. In 1984 they, as a group, registered a current account surplus of $1.8 billion (see Table 2.1).

Although the adjustment in the current account in 1982 and 1983 was achieved mainly through a sharp reduction in imports, it should be noted

25

Table 2.1   Current Account Surplus or Deficit of Argentina, Brazil, and Mexico, 1980-1984 (in billions of dollars)

Country	1980	1981	1982	1983	1984
Argentina	-4.8	-4.7	-2.3	-2.4	-2.5
Brazil	-12.5	-10.9	-14.7	-6.2	0.3
Mexico	-7.6	-14.0	-5.7	5.1	4.0
Total	-24.9	-29.6	-22.7	-3.5	1.8

Source: International Monetary Fund.

that imports *stopped* declining in 1983 and registered a small increase in 1984. It also should be remembered, of course, that the import levels of 1980 and 1981 were abnormally high and were hardly sustainable in the medium and long term.

The third area where progress can be reported is that relative to 1982 and 1983, global economic conditions have changed. The situation in industrial countries has improved considerably. In 1984, real output in industrial countries increased by almost 5 percent, the fastest pace in a decade and the volume of their imports increased by nearly 12 percent. Further, inflation has remained low, monetary conditions have eased, and interest rates have declined. To be sure, serious problems remain—and I refer to them later—but it can be concluded that world economic conditions are better today than in 1982 when real output was stagnant; the volumes of both industrial-country imports and world trade were declining; and inflation in the industrial countries was very high. Also, during 1984 and 1985, there was a recovery in the rate of economic growth of a good number of countries in Latin America (see Table 2.2).

Fourthly, it should not be overlooked that from the very beginning of the debt crisis, there was substantial international cooperation. All the parties involved—the authorities of both debtor and creditor countries and the financial institutions in both private and official sectors—responded in a quick and constructive manner. If one looks only at the financial role of the IMF in Latin America, it is worthwhile noting that between 1983 and 1984 it disbursed more than $10.5 billion (see Table 2.3). For comparison's sake, the IMF disbursed only $2.9 billion in the period 1975-1980.

The Present Situation

In 1986, a mixed picture emerges, of the world economy and of the indebted countries. More specifically, I draw your attention to the following three areas: the global economic environment; financial flows to indebted countries; and the continuity of the adjustment effort.

Table 2.2   Real GDP Growth in Argentina, Brazil, Chile, Mexico, and Venezuela, 1981-1984

Country	1981	1982	1983	1984	1985[a]
Argentina	-6.2	-5.2	-3.1	2.4	-3.0
Brazil	-1.6	0.9	-3.2	4.5	7.0
Chile	5.5	-14.1	-0.7	6.4	1.5
Mexico	7.9	-0.5	-5.3	3.7	3.9
Venezuela	0.3	0.7	-5.6	-1.4	-1.2

Source: International Monetary Fund.
[a] Estimated.

After an increase of 5 percent in 1984, growth in the industrial countries declined to about 3 percent in 1985. The rate of economic growth in the United States in 1985 (2.8 percent) was less than one-half what it had been (6.8 percent) in 1984. In Latin America, exports fell in 1985, compared to an increase of 10 percent in 1984. Of course, one of the most serious problems is the one faced by the oil-exporting countries of Latin America as a result of the sharp drop in the prices of oil. A preliminary calculation, based on an average price of $15 per barrel, indicates that Mexico, Venezuela, and Ecuador may see their combined oil export earnings come down by about $11 billion in 1986 from the $30 billion level of 1985. Given this context, it was very wise of the government of Venezuela to introduce a contingency clause in the restructuring agreement signed with the banks on February 26, 1986.

The second area of concern about the present situation has to do with the financial resources flowing to indebted countries. What is particularly worrisome is the rapid decline of net new commercial bank lending in 1985 in comparison to 1984. On a regional basis, international banks reduced their loans to countries in the western hemisphere by about $0.3 billion in the first three quarters of 1985, while they had lent $6.5 billion in the same period in 1984 and $14.9 billion in all of 1983.

Although it was desirable that the private international banks reduce the increases in their exposure from the unsustainable rates during the period 1978 to 1981, the extent to which their lending has slowed down now poses

Table 2.3   IMF Disbursements in Latin America, 1981-1985 (in billions of dollars)

Year	$
1981	561
1982	1,856
1983	6,609
1984	3,989
1985	1,863
	14,878

Source: International Monetary Fund.

a major problem. If this negative trend continues, it will constitute a very serious threat to the adjustment efforts of the indebted countries. Also, it is not clear how such limited development could be in the best interest of the commercial banks themselves. After all, it seems obvious—and only fair—that, to quote J. de Larosiere, "when adjustment programs are being implemented with courage and tenacity, it is essential that debtors be assured of continued understanding . . . on the part of their creditors."[1]

The end of 1985 saw a situation in which, unfortunately, a number of countries had reduced substantially the rate at which they were making progress. In a few instances, some countries had even lost ground in their efforts to adjust. This situation could be observed inter alia in the still-high budget deficits, the reduced domestic savings, and the persistence of inflation. The problem of inflation is particularly troublesome. Indeed, in Latin America, the average rate of inflation in 1985 was more than twice as high as it had been in 1982.

In this respect, it can be said that the adjustment process has been more successful in restoring external balance than in bringing about internal equilibrium. This result is not totally surprising; a substantial portion of external balance can be achieved without the intense political opposition engendered by actions to restore internal balance. Also, external balance can hardly be avoided because in the end, countries are forced to live within their external-resource availability. In other words, the restoration of a minimum of external balance is nearly inevitable as external financing dries up. Internal balance, in contrast, is not inevitable. To a large extent, it can be successfully postponed because authorities are able to retain some degree of freedom in the ways in which they deal with the size of fiscal deficits and the "acceptable" levels of inflation.

At the end of February 1986, Brazil adopted a commendable monetary reform. This action came after the rate of inflation had accelerated at year-end 1985 to extremely alarming levels. If one looks at this action together with what Argentina did in mid-July 1985 with its austral monetary reform, then it should be recognized that for most Latin American countries today, there is a new awareness of the risks and high costs of not controlling inflation. Yet, at the same time, one must say that overconfidence in dealing with inflation would be a serious mistake. After all, the control of inflation is only as durable as prudent fiscal and monetary policies are effective in dealing with inflation's root causes.

Policy Requirements for Durable Growth

The policy requirements to achieve sustained growth could be classified in three groups: economic policies within the indebted countries; the global economic environment; and adequate external financing. The most important of the three requirements is the economic policy of the indebted country. After all, even if the international economic environment were not the most auspicious or if the flows of external financing were to remain inadequate, experience demonstrates that those countries adopting the better economic policies will be better able to avoid the most onerous forms of adjustment.

But which policies bring forth growth and efficient adjustment? The key to achieve these objectives lies in increasing domestic savings, increasing public sector efficiency, increasing exports, and liberalizing foreign trade. Of these, I concentrate my attention on domestic savings as the most important factor. What determines growth? Most economists agree that durable growth is the consequence of higher investment, higher productivity, or a combination of the two.

How do you increase investment? How do you finance it? Here again, the answer is that higher investment is the result of higher savings. In its turn, higher productivity comes from more efficient allocation of resources, which is the essence of the Baker Initiative. But what are the sources of savings? The answer is that savings can come only from domestic or from external sources. At this juncture and during the next few years, Latin America will not be able—nor is it desirable—to finance a large part of its investment with external savings. It follows, then, that in order to maintain the previous levels of domestic investment, these countries need to increase their domestic savings. This is the only way to ensure that the adjustment effort leads the economy into sustained growth. Policy reform in the indebted countries cannot do the job alone. A favorable world economic climate also is necessary.

Without underestimating the immense immediate difficulties faced by the oil-exporting countries, one should be encouraged by two very important developments: the Baker Initiative and the Group of Five agreement of September 22, 1985. These two events should not be regarded as isolated actions. On the contrary, they mutually reinforce each other, and they both share the same basic philosophy. The objectives of the Group of Five agreement—continued and more balanced growth in the industrial countries and an orderly depreciation of the U.S. dollar—are precisely the conditions needed to boost the sagging export earnings of the debtor countries to which the Baker Initiative is addressed.

One concrete result of the support given to the Baker Initiative is the decision taken by the IMF's board of directors on March 26, 1986, to establish a structural adjustment facility (SAF) to provide balance-of-payments assistance to sixty low-income countries eligible for the International Development Association (IDA) resources. This facility is financed by special drawing rights (SDR) of $2.7 billion that will become available during the period 1985-1991 from repayments of IMF trust fund loans. The utilization of this facility will result in an improvement in the economic performance of those countries and thus will contribute to the establishment of a more favorable world economic climate.

In brief, the global economic environment, although somewhat mixed because of the growing and severe problems faced by oil-exporting countries, could be described as generally favorable. Surely, no one can predict the future, and, of course, indebted countries must be able to find markets for their exports if they are to be successful in their adjustment efforts. On the whole, however, I would say that the world economic climate is *now* auspicious to the implementation of a workable debt strategy.

We need to ensure adequate external financing for those countries making progress in their adjustment efforts. Without such financing, growth, adjustment, and, ultimately, the servicing of the existing debt will suffer. Unfortunately, the net flows from the international banks to Latin America actually went *down* in three quarters of 1985.

To be sure, the recent multiyear rescheduling arrangements have been of considerable benefit, but it is also true that some lending packages have been difficult to put together even where strong programs of adjustment were in place. This difficulty has persisted even when the creditors are able to convert an original claim on the *private* sector of the indebted country into a more secure and valuable claim on the *public* sector of the same country. This is a very important point. Not only is new commercial money still needed, but it should be forthcoming without further burdening the public sectors of the indebted countries. After all, when public sectors assume as their own risk what was originally a private risk, they in fact are increasing their present or future fiscal costs.

The Baker Initiative

In his address to the 1985 annual meetings of the IMF and the World Bank at Seoul, U.S. Treasury Secretary James Baker proposed a "program for sustained growth" to strengthen the present international debt strategy. The first element in his proposal was the adoption by debtor countries of comprehensive macroeconomic and structural policies to promote growth and balance-of-payments adjustment and reduce inflation. The second element was a continued central role for the IMF, in conjunction with more effective lending by multilateral development banks. The third was increased lending by the private banks in support of comprehensive adjustment programs.

One specific aspect of the Baker Initiative is particularly relevant and timely. I refer to the complementariness of demand-management policies, on the one hand, and supply-side policies, on the other, in an effort to bring about both external equilibrium and the restoration of sustainable growth.

To the well-established principle that adjustment is a *sine qua non* condition for the resolution of the debt problem, Secretary Baker has added a particular dimension or component of growth, not so much from corrective demand-management policies, but from remedial supply-side policies.

The proposal assumes, and rightly so, that there is a given amount of growth that can be derived from measures and policies that mainly restore external equilibrium, but that if sustainable growth or substantial reduction of inflation also is sought as a main objective, then additional and concrete policy actions are required to correct structural rigidities on the supply side. A country can achieve a considerable degree of external adjustment and still retain a large degree of internal inefficiency. To remove these inefficiencies, which are obstacles to long-term growth, specific action is required in such areas as trade liberalization, interest rates, savings, and wage indexation.

The broad questions of the size of the public sector and of public sector efficiency lie at the bottom of any effort to sustain growth in the medium term. The issues here are very fundamental. It is not only that fiscal deficits should come down, but that they should do so through cutbacks in expenditures rather than through raised revenues. Furthermore, the cuts in expenditures should be made in current expenditures and not in productive investment. Privatization schemes should be adopted, and the whole macroeconomic framework within which they are to operate must change.

Within this context, the Baker Initiative is clearly more ambitious than a mere stabilization plan for external adjustment. It poses a profound challenge to policymakers. The scope for incurrence of external imbalance, in the last analysis, is inevitable, while internal adjustment—that is cutting fiscal deficits, bringing down inflation, and increasing domestic savings—is more the result of deliberate discretionary action on the part of the authorities. Actions of this latter type are more difficult to adopt; they are not necessarily inevitable. But if sustained growth is the first priority, then supply-side policy actions are unavoidable.

Over the medium term, if structural inefficiencies remain, demand-managed policies alone cannot restore both external balance and sustained growth. By bringing out these two complementary policies and emphasizing the need to act vigorously on both fronts, the Baker Initiative has made a very significant contribution to the understanding and resolution of the debt problem over the medium and long term.

Notes

The views presented here are those of the author and do not necessarily represent the position of the International Monetary Fund.

1. J. de Larosiere, speech delivered at the annual Spring Membership Meeting of the Institute of International Finance, Washington, D.C., May 10, 1986, p. 6.

chapter three

The Costs for Latin America's Development

Jésus Silva-Herzog

The bottom line of the debt crisis is the cost to Latin America in terms of development—or rather, judging by recent evidence, the *lack* of development.

Development always has been understood as a concept that is broader than mere growth. It encompasses the quality of life, the general level of welfare; it implies the degree to which men and women can pursue and fulfill their dreams and ambitions. It is *about* men and women and their families. Let us always remember that behind the neutral figures we review lie people's lives, which are the real concern of development.

In appraising the cost of the debt crisis to Latin America's development, it is very helpful, first, to look at the origins of the debt and then at the associated attitudes adopted by the different actors in the world since 1982.

The Origins of the Crisis

The origin of the debt itself is clearly traceable to a decision by both developing and developed countries that, although guided by different motivations, resulted in the channeling of tens of billions of dollars to the debtor community of today. Developing countries wanted and needed to grow, and developed countries found themselves holding large amounts of money that they could not absorb. The developed countries actively promoted the so-called "recycling" of this liquidity, and it ended up as the debt of developing nations. The whole world congratulated itself on the success, smoothness, and efficiency with which the recycling process was achieved. *We all were responsible.*

The economic outlook in the early 1970s also was good. Both borrowers and lenders shared a belief that there would remain continued growth in developing countries, remunerative prices for raw materials, and low interest rates. The accumulation of a large amount of debt seemed natural. The yield of each project would permit the repayment of the debt.

But then the world changed. As industrial countries abandoned the commitment to growth in favor of the fight against inflation, the locomotives of the world's growth lost steam. This was not in the original plans. Neither was the steady deterioration of the terms of trade of developing countries, as their exports failed to find a home in a world no longer hungry for them. The unprecedented rise in interest rates that followed the anti-inflation strategy of industrial countries also was absent in our original collective view of the future.

Yet governments of developing countries clung to their original goal of development, even in the face of clear evidence that these negative changes were not just temporary distortions but rather the structural result of forces beyond government control. Expectations had been raised. Governments received mandates based on the promise of a better life ahead, and they had little choice but to continue promoting growth policies in order to deliver what they had offered.

Suddenly the whole world was again acting in unison, but the motivations were different. The world still was channeling resources to developing countries in large amounts, but the lenders were no longer doing so to recycle surplus liquidity, but rather to protect the assets they had created in the past. The borrowers were borrowing more, but no longer to promote development; rather, they continued to borrow merely to be able to pay. We collectively got deeper and deeper into the debt crisis. We all were responsible.

But once the debt crisis became apparent in the summer of 1982, the shared responsibility for the origin of the problem was fundamentally ignored. It is true that we have avoided a collapse of the financial system; it is also true that we have been able to "muddle through" since 1982 without major shocks or confrontations. But the cost has been heavy, and it has not been shared in a manner consistent with the shared responsibility for the creation of the problem. The cost to debtor countries has been high. In particular, the cost in terms of Latin America's development has been extremely onerous.

The Costs of "Adjustment"

Let me mention only a few examples of this cost, which has been euphemistically described as "adjustment." The volume of goods and services that

Latin America needs to export in 1986 in order to finance the import of a given volume of merchandise from developed countries is 20 percent higher than in 1980, given the deterioration of the terms of trade; *Latin Americans sell more and get less.* The case of oil-exporting countries is particularly dramatic. In 1986, Mexico lost one-third of its exports of merchandise, more than $6 billion, solely through the decline in oil income. Other countries were affected similarly.

By the end of 1985, Latin America needed more than one-third of its total exports to pay interest on the debt, against one-fifth in 1980. From 1983 to 1985, the region transferred abroad more than $105 billion in interest payments and profit remittances. It only received $18 billion in loans and new investments. Banks halted lending abruptly in a reaction that was as mechanical and inflexible as the one that inspired their original lending spree. Potential equity investors in the area also balked. They did not want to invest in countries with payment problems and low growth prospects. It all became a self-fulfilling prophecy—no new resources caused further payments problems, which scared away other *potential* new resources.

Not surprisingly, however, the distribution of the costs of the debt crisis was determined largely by the reaction of the different actors to the crisis itself. Although this might sound tautological, it is worth stressing because it has produced a completely lopsided pattern of burden-sharing.

Banks adopted the attitude that debtors should continue to fully service their debts in exchange for stretching their maturities. No substantive sacrifice was involved, except for rather modest reductions in spreads for some of the debtor countries.

Governments of industrial countries adopted the attitude that banks were imprudent institutions that should pay for their sins and did not deserve any relief, either regulatory or material. This obviously made banks' lives more difficult and, by extension, debtors' lives almost impossible. The warm praise banks got from their governments for their efficiency in the recycling process a few years earlier suddenly turned to sharp criticism.

Debtor countries, in contrast, acted with great responsibility. The continued need of foreign savings, the growing international economic interdependence, and a legitimate desire to honor their obligations as a matter of principle led them to pay *full interest* in exchange for stretching maturities. Confrontation was systematically avoided in the hope that an improvement in the external environment would bail the debtor countries out.

Debtor countries also accepted IMF-supported domestic adjustment policies. These adjustment policies became a necessary precondition for debtor countries before banks would lend new money. The belt-tightening was impressive. A few figures clearly show it. On the external sector, imports dropped by one-third from their 1980 level of $90 billion; in 1986, they remained below $60 billion for all of Latin America. Exports, however, re-mained steady from 1980 to 1985 at $90 billion per year, despite volume increases and given price deterioration. Exports declined to $78 billion in 1986 because of sharp reductions in oil and grain prices. The much heralded improvement in Latin America's current accounts therefore is attributable mostly to import reduction, rather than to export increase. By year-end 1986, a current account deficit of approximately $5.7 billion emerged for the area as a whole, with oil exporters the most affected.

The domestic adjustment also was substantial and painful. In terms of development, the price was heavy indeed. Real cumulative growth for the area from 1980 to 1985 was only 2.3 percent; in fact, if Brazil and Cuba are excluded, the figure is only 0.4 percent. This implies a negative per capita growth of almost 9 percent for all of Latin America and of 11.4 percent excluding Brazil and Cuba.

The implications in terms of real wages, employment, and welfare in general are only too obvious. The social and political implications also should be obvious. But there are also ethical questions involved. The original conviction that the repayment of a debt incurred was almost a matter of national pride clearly is being substituted by the overriding need to provide Latin American societies with a minimum level of welfare. The debt problem, which is viewed basically as purely financial in the industrial countries, already has become an essential political problem in debtor nations.

To make matters worse, the debt problem today continues to be exacerbated by the tenacity of high real rates of interest and the constantly deteriorating terms of trade. Thus, the proverbial light at the end of the tunnel seems permanently occluded.

There is an old saying that if you get to the end of your rope, you should tie a knot and hang on. But hanging on is precisely what developing countries in Latin America have been doing since 1982 in the expectation that concerted international effort might bring about a favorable change in outlook. So far, this effort has failed to materialize.

Sharing the Burdens of Debt:
An Ethical, Moral, and Pragmatic Response

We all must persevere in our efforts to resolve the debt crisis using a new approach that makes burden-sharing more equitable. We must participate in a more definite solution to the debt problem; the costs and sacrifices involved should be shared by creditors and debtors alike. Interest rate relief, regulatory relief, sufficient new credit, access for Latin American exports at remunerative prices—these niceties are no longer merely desirable but essential. They have become a precondition to any efficient, nonconfrontational solution to the debt crisis.

The Group of Five decision to devalue the dollar, the recent concerted reduction in interest rates, and the launching of a new trade round all prove that governments can intervene successfully to direct the course of events, instead of simply resigning themselves to the workings of an invisible hand.

The plight of the oil-exporting, heavily indebted countries recently has provided a case in point. For the industrial countries, the drop in oil prices probably did more to enhance the prospect of growth, low interest rates, and low inflation than any consensual efforts among the big economies of the world to date. On balance, the oil price drop even implies an advantage for banks and a net enhancement of the quality of their total assets. Most developing countries are also better off.

These statements by an official of the country that has been hardest hit by the drop in oil prices may sound bizarre. But they reflect an inescapable reality. It is also true, however, that if only a fraction of these benefits accruing to creditor banks and creditor countries could be channeled to the debtors that are most affected—for example, through interest costs and compensatory financing in adequate terms—the economic, social, and political dangers posed by further deterioration of the debt crisis could be relieved significantly.

Meanwhile, sacrificing development for the sake of stability can be only a temporary strategy, not an end in itself. Development is the only answer to the debt problem—and today, the debt problem is one of the major roadblocks to development. We must break this vicious circle in order to allow development to happen. Therefore, we must deal more decisively with the debt. We must create the necessary global atmosphere, provide sound regulatory accounting and a workable mechanical framework, and cultivate a more profound, more political vision to avoid unnecessary pain and conflict.

The responsible attitude from Latin America, through the Cartagena Group, shows the seriousness and maturity with which an important group of debtor countries is reacting to this fundamental challenge. Such cooperation—both among debtor countries and between debtors and lenders—was always the best way; it is now the only way. It is politically and socially indispensable, and it is ethically and morally right. In a world dominated by pragmatism, we always must remind ourselves that relying on such fundamental values still remains the only legitimate and lasting approach to today's problems.

chapter four

The Threat to Democracy

Daniel Oduber

Latin American democracy always has been conditioned by extraregional powers and events. Since 1940, U.S. foreign policy has been the most important external element, but recently the debt crisis has begun to affect the prospects for the maintenance or expansion of democracy. Let me offer a brief historical overview of the history of democracy in Latin America and then discuss the impact of the debt crisis on democracy.

The Emergence of Democracy

During World War II, some of the Allied powers expended great efforts to convince all countries of the importance of democracy and human rights. Their effective campaign against totalitarianism in Europe and in Asia bore fruit. In April 1945, the United Nations, founded on the principles of human rights, was established in San Francisco. All new countries struggling for freedom based their demands on U.N. documents and on the promises and propaganda of World War II. The United Nations announced clearly that democracy was the ideal government of the future.

Latin American countries had been struggling to achieve democracy and freedom since independence, but with very few exceptions had not been successful. However, I must emphasize that there were many citizens in each of the countries who became outstanding leaders in the area of human rights.

These movements to create the necessary conditions for democracy in Latin America were supported in the United States and in Europe. Slowly, a crusade for democracy developed in the Western world. Old *caudillo* dictators weakened and lost power in their own countries, and as technology and communications improved understanding among the American states, dictators found it increasingly difficult to maintain power. To survive, these dictators recognized the need to appear "modern" and democratic.

In 1950, a group of statesmen from Latin America and the United States met in Havana, Cuba, to discuss what they could do to promote democracy and freedom in the hemisphere. This critical meeting stimulated others, involving senators, representatives, trade union leaders, writers, and politicians of the two Americas to coordinate efforts to fight for human rights in the continent. In time, a permanent relationship among some leaders and groups of the Americas was established to promote democracy and to offer hope to the masses of Latin America.

In the Eisenhower years, Vice President Nixon was insulted and humiliated in Latin America because he was perceived as an ally of the dictators. He was an open defender of economic interests subservient to these dictators. The insults caused a reassessment of policies. President Eisenhower commissioned his brother, Milton, to review relations between the countries of Latin America and the United States. Two former Latin American presidents, Juscelino Kubitschek of Brazil and Alberto Lleras Camargo of Colombia, were selected to present ideas to the Eisenhower administration.

Months of meetings, studies, and deliberations gave rise to ideas that crystallized into a new approach to the relationship. Economic development was seen as an indispensable element in the modernization of a Latin America that desperately needed social and political change. The Inter-American Development Bank was created, and new, aggressive development programs began.

However, parallel to these developments, the deepening of the Cold War between Soviet Russia and the Western democracies began to affect U.S. policy toward Latin America. Dictators continued to weaken, but the radicalization of Castro's Cuba and its move into the Soviet bloc gave temporary relief to those dictators who were considered by some policymakers to be good friends of the United States. The true fighters for democracy were considered dangerous by reactionary forces in the United States, and the long struggle for democracy lost ground.

During the Kennedy years (the early 1960s), there were many enlightened U.S. political leaders giving great support to those Latin American leaders who were involved permanently in the fight for democracy. Very little support was given to dictators during these years. Whenever a coup d'etat was executed against a democratic president, the new government was neither recognized nor supported in any way by Washington. To be a dictator in the early 1960s was to be against Washington. A massive economic effort undertaken at the same time—the Alliance for Progress—stimulated modernization and a number of social programs, such as land reform, which were supported by the United States.

The majority of Latin American countries were democracies in those years. Also, a group of Caribbean states (former European colonies) with a democratic tradition inherited from the colonial era became independent. Democracy and development became inseparable. Virtually all the efforts undertaken by pro-Castro communist groups in the region failed.

The Vietnam War unfortunately changed the mentality of many leaders in the United States. The specter of Cuba again became a major element in the making of foreign policy. Many young officers of Latin American armies had been trained in the United States. Their studies were no longer limited to military training but extended to government policy, economics, and international relations. Many of the officers came to believe that they were the only reliable group in Latin America able to stop communism and to guarantee serious, honest, and efficient governments. Slowly, the true representatives of Latin American democratic societies were eliminated (some of them physically), and a new wave of military regimes took over that did not stop communism—far from it—but destroyed the decades of effort to build modern democracies in Latin America.

Destruction and Restoration . . .

By the middle of the 1970s, few democracies were left. The international crises of the 1970s found, with very few exceptions, a Latin America governed by generals. What is even sadder, the 1970s found many civilian presidents in Latin America unable to say no to the military or to resist unnecessary government expenditures. The financial, energy, and food crises of the 1970s became additional forces in this trend to destroy the democratic institutions of Latin America.

The Carter administration made an extraordinary effort in the late 1970s to encourage democratic restoration in Latin America. The administration's pursuit of human rights policies convinced many military dictators to return to their barracks, thereby strengthening democratic leaders and encouraging them to take over. Once more, democracy became the wave of the hemisphere. Countries that had been under dictatorships for decades found themselves again learning the rules of a democratic society.

But it had become more difficult in the 1980s. These societies had been brutally suppressed for many years. The economy was in ruins, and social conditions were deplorable. During the short revival of democracies in the 1950s and 1960s, these societies had begun to awaken, and the demands of the poorest sectors were being addressed. By the 1980s, the postponed demands were overwhelming, but the economies, unfortunately, were in ruins.

The financial, energy, and food crises occurred when most of the Latin American countries had very weak governments, which had grown accustomed to borrowing and spending. Credit was offered generously. Safeguards to ensure that loans would be serviced were disregarded. The world was floating on oil dollars, and bankers convinced many generals to sign loans for unnecessary projects.

. . . and Debt

The legacy left to democratic leaders in Latin America cannot be described easily. In addition to the problems of countries dependent on a few export products for their foreign exchange, a reduction of world commodity prices (caused by a drop in world demand) aggravated the crisis. The gap had to be filled with loans. Increasingly expensive oil imports were financed by loans. Rising expectations from the middle and lower classes meant the necessity of more infrastructure, and this was satisfied by loans. Social services had to be financed by budget deficits, and all these had to be met by money issues, by loans, or by both.

The political and social implications of the external debt became the principal problem of the fragile new democracies. Established democracies, on the other hand, were better equipped to deal with social protest and economic stagnation because they already had created the necessary mechanisms to meet such crises. In fact, social organizations and political institutions *have* been able to meet the difficult problems created by this debt since 1980. However, in spite of this semipreparedness, the pressure continues to rise.

The oil-producing countries in the area overspent in the good years, creating subsidy mechanisms that could not contract easily when the price of oil declined. The result, as in the other countries, was unemployment and unrest. It was because of these impoverished classes that the germ of revolution began to spread again.

There is a marked tendency today in most Latin American countries to improve democratic institutions. But in some cases the task has become impossible due to the regressive measures that must be taken by new democratic governments. Moreover, the incomprehensible recommendations of international agency bureaucrats who want to apply similar measures in all cases—without the necessary social and historical distinctions—may provoke a serious, perhaps chaotic situation soon.

True Democracy Must Be Renewed

It is not easy to create democracy in a Latin American country that has little experience with it. Democracy demands many years of preparation and education, but in order to have education we must free funds that are now devoted solely to meeting the demands of the external debt or to supporting defense expenditures that serve mostly to suppress the just demands of impoverished populations.

The building of democratic institutions will take at least a generation in some countries. It is expensive. Considering the economic restrictions some international organizations want to apply, it may be impossible to educate these populations to build solid democracies.

For some foreign observers the mere celebration of elections is proof of democracy. Nothing could be further from the truth. Absolutely the most dangerous thing today in young societies is to confuse democracy with elections. Democracy is a very difficult and long process that has to begin in the school and in the family. Democracy is discredited when dictators hold elections but allow exploitation and hunger.

Reducing expenditures for the military and increasing them for health and education should be the basis of democracy in the hemisphere. But the external debt is leaving Latin America without the necessary funds to educate or to protect the ill and also without the necessary investment money to create jobs and to modernize the economies.

To provide Latin America funds only to pay debts does no service to democracy. On the contrary, to offer funds under these circumstances is to freeze the social problems and to gradually undermine democratic recovery. Countries that do not respect human rights should be placed in a category that would limit their access to economic aid until they accept this ethical basis of development. It is only with a general program of recovery—including, of course, reasonable payments on the debt—that Latin America can meet its social and political needs.

Latin American history has taught us that unemployment breeds guerrillas and that once a revolution begins, only dictators of the right or of the left can prevail. To believe that dictatorships, once established, are more likely to pay their debts is infantile, just as it was infantile to make loans to such regimes in the beginning.

chapter five

The Environmental Dimension to the Debt Crisis: The Problem and Five Proposals

J. Gustave Speth

To many policymakers trying to cope with the international debt crisis, resource and environmental deterioration must seem largely irrelevant or perhaps an unfortunate sidelight. This perspective is flawed, and I develop three points that explain why.

First, the natural resource sectors loom very large in the economies of developing countries in general and debtor countries in particular, and increased production from careful management in these sectors can provide an important part of the answer to the debt crisis. Second, contrary to what one would hope, the natural resource base in most of the Third World is not being managed for sustainable production today, and long-term growth prospects are being diminished by resource deterioration, a deterioration that the debt crisis seems to be hastening. Third, there are important steps that can and should be taken to make the resource sectors become less of the problem and more of the solution.

The Goal: Economic Growth

The premise of Secretary James A. Baker's plan unveiled in 1985 at Seoul was that sustained economic growth, not IMF-imposed austerity, offers the only genuine hope for an improvement in the fortunes of debtor nations and for the end of a threat to the U.S. financial system. The solution to the current predicament is to grow out of it.

The prospects for sustained economic growth are affected mightily by what happens in the resource sectors—agriculture, fisheries, forests, energy, and minerals—of Third World countries. These sectors generate at least half of the gross national product (GNP) in many developing and debtor countries and account for even larger shares of employment. They account typically for more than half of all exports and almost half of imports. The rediscovery of these sectors has been one of the more notable, and hopeful, features of recent development thinking. Farmers, not industrial tycoons, increasingly are seen as pivotal figures.

Twenty-five years ago, the accumulation of capital was thought to be the key to growth. The human contribution was the supply of labor—usually in surplus in the developing countries. The multilateral development banks (MDBs) invested in power plants and highways, and most developing countries embarked on excessively capital-intensive development plans. The World Bank later played an important role in demonstrating the economic returns to investments in people—in the form of higher productivity. Large-scale investments in health, nutrition, and education followed. A similar intellectual shift now is needed to demonstrate the returns from investments in natural resource productivity.

A key question is how to resume steady growth where there are only limited prospects for increasing external finance. A key answer is to manage locally available natural resources well. Achieving large, sustained productivity increases from the existing resource base and making more efficient use of petroleum and other imported resources can make a real difference. A few examples illustrate the point.

- About 15 percent of debtor country imports are for food. Improvements in domestic agricultural productivity are needed to meet the needs of expanding populations, and, as the examples of India and China make clear, these improvements can markedly improve trade balances. Even where net food exports are not a realistic possibility, reductions in food imports are.

- A good example of making better use of available resources is in the area of irrigated agriculture. The Food and Agriculture Organization anticipates investments of $100 billion throughout the rest of the century to expand irrigated areas, but if current irrigated areas attained their production potential through better management, only limited expansion would be needed.

- Another 15 percent of imports by developing countries is for fuel, and a generous share of external financing has gone to hydro and other power projects. Yet, all available studies indicate that the potential for sharp improvements in energy efficiency in developing countries—from Brazil to Kenya—is enormous and represents the least costly approach to balancing energy supply and demand. Also, in many countries, biomass energy systems offer excellent promise in reducing oil imports.

• Surprisingly, developing country imports of forest products exceed $10 billion annually and are increasing steadily. Many countries (such as Mexico and Nigeria) that should be able to supply their own needs are major importers. In other countries, industrial forestry has been neglected to the point that exports are in decline.

My point is that the more effective use of locally available resources suggested by these examples can simultaneously reduce the need for foreign investment, save and earn foreign exchange, expand domestic production, and reduce resource deterioration.

The Problem: Mismanagement and Resource Deterioration

Thus far, I intentionally have stressed in rather rosy terms the positive contribution that improved natural resource management can make to ameliorating the debt crisis. I believe firmly that the potential is there, but if it is to be realized, some important changes must be made. The sad facts are that resource deterioration is proceeding apace in most of the Third World today; prospects for long-term, sustained growth are being reduced; development assistance projects and policies have contributed to these negative trends; and the debt crisis and the measures adopted to cope with it have tended to make things worse—some would argue *much* worse. Too often the prospects for debt servicing are being undermined, not strengthened, by what is going on in the resource sectors, and short-sighted responses to the debt crisis are themselves part of the problem.

Today, the Third World is in the midst of a resource deterioration crisis that may be more significant in the long run than the foreign debt crisis. Deforestation in the tropics is claiming an area the size of Austria annually, and loss of forest-based livelihoods, soil erosion, downstream flooding, siltation, and the disappearance of species and genetic resources are among the typical consequences. The effects ripple through agriculture, energy supply, and water quality, adversely affecting the lives of about 1 billion people living in the tropics. Simultaneously, the existing crop and range land base in arid and semiarid regions is being diminished steadily. The U.N. estimates that moderate to severe "decertification" now affects 60 percent of productive lands in these regions. In countries as diverse as Haiti and Guatemala, Turkey, and India, erosion has curtailed sharply the country's agricultural potential, sometimes by 50 percent or more.

The underlying causes of these and other pressures on the Third World's resource base are many and complex. To mention a few:

- Rapid population growth, combined with mass poverty
- Modernization's disruption of traditional methods of environmental management and social control
- Various economic policies pursued by governments both North and South, including improper pricing and tax policies for energy, water, forest products, and agriculture
- Misguided development and aid policies, including support of large-scale development schemes that neglect both the environmental setting and local needs

The director of Earthscan, the international news service, has stressed this last point in blunt terms: "A great deal of development in the Third World—perhaps most of it—does not work. It is quite simply a waste of money, because it is not environmentally sound, and is therefore not sustainable."[1]

The Third World landscape is littered with development projects, often capital-intensive megaprojects like large dams and irrigation schemes, that produce far short of intended returns because of poor environmental and social planning.

One would presume that because of the debt crisis and the shortage of capital, proposals for new, large, capital-intensive development projects would be getting more careful scrutiny today. But what one hears repeatedly from Latin American and other observers is that the debt crisis is slowly undermining hard-fought recent gains in resource conservation and environmental protection. Although available information is mainly anecdotal, the following points are frequently made:

- Conservation always take a back seat in times of economic stress. As economic conditions have worsened in developing countries, and as debt pressures mount, there has been a tendency to ignore environmental planning and conservation measures in both industrial and rural development projects.
- The austerity measures that have been required include government cutbacks in both staffs and expenditures. These fall disproportionately on fledgling, weak environmental and conservation agencies and programs. This is undermining the early efforts that have been made to bring ecological considerations into development planning and projects.
- Austerity measures and general recessionary conditions also have led to sharp declines in per capita incomes and increases in unemployment. This puts more pressure on the natural resource base as more people rely directly on it.
- Pressures to expand primary commodity exports can lead to increased deforestation and to expansion of cash cropping on available

good lands, thus further marginalizing the rural poor and forcing them to poorer, erosion-prone lands.

In concluding, I would like to buttress these arguments with two points that are more environmental in the traditional sense. First, air and water-pollution have now reached crisis levels in many areas of the Third World; the public health costs alone—for example, those in Mexico City—are staggering. Only shortsighted policies will allow the debt situation to excuse environmental cleanup. Second, the industrial countries have a great stake in the preservation of the biological diversity and genetic richness of the poorer countries of the tropics. Without elaborating the many reasons for preserving species in their natural habitats, let me just note that the loss of these habitats is a major part of the natural resource crisis occurring today in the Third World.

The Solution: Managing the Natural Resources, Managing the Debt

If our goal is to make resource conditions in debtor countries part of the solution rather than part of the problem, then the needed policy measures must address both the previous problems of inadequate attention to resources and the environment, and the newer problems of debt crisis-induced shortsightedness. Here are five specific measures aimed at these objectives.

1. The twin goals of improved natural resource management and environmentally sensitive development must be injected into efforts to restructure and reschedule debts. More attention should be given to the natural resource and environmental implications of economic policy changes that are recommended or adopted to restore financial balance. IMF and other "conditionality" requirements should seek affirmatively to preserve programs that prevent irreversible environmental and resource damage. Both those imposing and those implementing austerity measures should exempt such programs from the budget axe.

2. Increased external financing for development in debt-ridden countries should be made available from both public and private sources, but all U.S. and multilateral programs providing or encouraging these funds should insist on improved natural resource management and on development that is environmentally sensitive and sustainable. World Bank structural adjustment lending and other policy-oriented, nonproject lending should seek explicit policy changes that recognize that degradation of natural resources results in serious economic and other losses and undermines development

programs. There is a long agenda of policy changes that simultaneously could move developing countries toward more sustainable use of natural resources *and* more sustainable fiscal balance. Among these policies, I call particular attention to eliminating price distortions and subsidies that encourage wasteful exploitation of forest, water, and energy resources.

3. Multilateral development banks and development assistance agencies should upgrade sharply their scrutiny of development projects, thus protecting against poor environmental and social planning that could shorten project life, reduce economic returns, or cause costly environmental damage. Simultaneously, the United States and other industrial countries should initiate serious new efforts aimed at helping developing countries upgrade their *own* environmental and resource management capabilities. An impressive program to do this was recently proposed by the Congressional Environmental and Energy Study Institute.[2]

4. A larger portion of total development assistance should go to meet large unmet investment needs that can improve sharply the productivity of the resource sectors: reforestation and fuelwood development, watershed protection, soil conservation, agroforestry, bioenergy, rehabilitation of existing irrigation projects, small-scale agriculture, and low-cost sanitation measures. Experience has shown that the most effective projects of this type are smaller-scale projects with a maximum grass-roots participation. A major new plan to counter the negative forces of deforestation recently has been developed by the World Bank, the United Nations Development Program, and the World Resources Institute.

5. Building on existing provisions in PL-480 and Section 124 of the Foreign Assistance Act, debts owed to the U.S. government by the poorest of the poor (about thirty-six least-developed countries, mostly in Africa) should be allowed to be "repaid" in local currencies and the funds so generated then made available for small-scale agricultural, biological conservation, and other specified development projects in the debtor country. Relatedly, consideration should be given to a program allowing the debts of the poorest of the poor to be written down or off (i.e., settled) as part of a structural adjustment package. Both these measures respond to the idea that for a group of extremely poor countries, insisting on debt payments is almost certainly counterproductive.

These five points, then, are realistic—and even attainable—steps toward managing the debt through better management of the natural resources of the Third World. No one approach offers the complete answer to these countries' problems, of course. But by now it should be obvious to all—lender and debtor countries alike—that wise resource management and environmental sensitivity, combined with other more financially and economically oriented measures, are unarguably logical bases from which to start.

Notes

1. Jon Tinker, "On the Side of the Future" (London: Earthscan, 1984), pp. 1, 3.

2. Environmental and Energy Study Institute, "A Congressional Agenda for Improved Resource and Environmental Management in the Third World: Helping Developing Countries Help Themselves" (Washington, D.C.: Environmental and Energy Study Institute, October 1985).

chapter six

The Threat to the International Banking System

Terence C. Canavan

The impact of the developing country problem on commercial banks is a subject about which there is a great deal of misunderstanding, concern, and confusion. There are those who believe that the debt burden imposed on the developing countries already has inflicted irreversible and, in a sense, terminal damage on both the borrowing countries and their commercial bank creditors. On the other hand, there are numerous recent reports that imply that the debt problems of many developing countries essentially have been resolved.

As is usually the case, the truth lies between these two analyses. It would be naive and dangerous to assume that the debt problem is in the past, that the creditworthiness of the developing countries has been restored, and that developing country debt exposure poses no special problem for the commercial banks. But it would be equally wrong to assume that the problems of the international financial system are insoluble. A solution satisfactory to both the borrowing countries and their creditors will require careful management and close cooperation by all: developing country borrowers, official lenders, and commercial banks. A solution also will require appropriate economic policies in the industrial countries and their direct involvement with the debt problem.

The Nature of the Problem

To understand the impact of the debt on the commercial banks, it is necessary to understand the fundamental nature of the issue. Some observers accuse the banks of trying to camouflage their problems and hide them from the public and the shareholders. In the view of these critics, the developing-country loans on the banks' books should be acknowledged as losses and simply written off—with all that implies for profitability and for the banks themselves. Let me explain why this view is mistaken.

The debt problem already has had a profound impact on the banks. But good management and close cooperation by all involved will prevent far more serious shocks to the international financial system than those we have seen thus far. In my view, it is appropriate to assess what already has happened, but it is far more important to learn from our experiences, halt the erosion that has occurred up to this point, and restore the developing countries to a state of solid economic and financial health.

In August 1982, Jésus Silva-Herzog, Mexico's minister of finance, announced that Mexico would not be able to continue the service of its debt without the aid of special measures. What has happened since is very well known. The immediate impact on the commercial banks was a cessation of their business-as-usual lending approach to the financially troubled borrowers. However controversial this reaction may have seemed, it is best understood, I think, as a logical extension of the historical context in which banks and developing countries had been working for decades.

With or Without Oil: Different Debt Patterns

During the 1960s, long-term loans to the non-oil-exporting developing countries increased at the rapid rate of 16 percent per year. However, because of its low initial base, the outstanding long-term debt of these countries at year-end 1973 stood at just less than $100 billion. Approximately one-half of that debt was held by official creditors, and only a little more than one-third was held by the commercial banks.

During the next nine years, the long-term debt of non-OPEC (Organization of Petroleum Exporting Countries) developing countries grew at an average rate of 19 percent. By the end of 1982, that debt totaled $480 billion. The relative share of official creditors in the debt of the non-oil-exporting developing countries had fallen to less than 40 percent, while the commercial banks' share had risen to more than 50 percent. Much of this rapid accumulation of external debt was associated with the financing of oil-inflated external deficits. The surplus and the aggregate current account of the oil-exporting developing countries increased by a factor of more than ten in 1974. The mirror image of this development, perhaps not surprisingly, was an almost fourfold increase in the current account deficit of the non-oil-developing countries.

As a result of these developments, the international financial system quickly focused on the problem of recycling petrodollars. As official lenders were unwilling or unable to take on this added responsibility, the international commercial banks stepped forward and became the major link in pet-rodollar recycling. In some ways, this recycling effort was a natural extension of what the banks, long accustomed to doing business with developing countries, already were doing.

The strategy of financing current account deficits through the recycling of petrodollars worked extremely well for some time. The growth of output in the major non-oil developing countries slowed along with the rest of the world economy in 1975; however, helped by strong commodity prices and vigorous growth in world trade, the developing countries sustained a burst of growth in 1976 and remained strong through 1978—stronger, in fact, than growth in the industrial countries. Even more impressive was the fact that developing countries' external deficits stabilized after 1975 and even declined through 1978.

Brazil illustrates this pattern clearly. In 1972, oil accounted for only 12 percent of Brazil's imports; by 1978, that figure had risen to 31 percent, an increase in relative share of 158 percent. The impact of the 1973–1974 oil price increases was even greater in terms of Brazil's marginal borrowing requirements. But facilitated by foreign loans, Brazil's economy grew in real terms from 1973 through 1980 at an average annual rate of about 7 percent—high by any standard.

Even with the heavy borrowing that occurred through the 1970s, by 1979 the debt service ratio of the developing world as a whole was approximately 19 to 22 percent. Historically, the banking community has considered any ratio less than 20 percent to be moderate and in no way alarming. Furthermore, the petrodollar lending was long term. Had we realized in 1980 that we had a serious problem, it would have been foolhardy to withdraw before trying to resolve it in some orderly way.

The Late 1970s: Unforeseen Shocks

There are some who believe that the actions by the banks that resulted in the buildup of loans were foolish and that only now have the banks come to their senses. In contrast, I think it can be demonstrated that the present difficulties resulted from a number of developments that hardly could have been anticipated. Even now, with the full benefits of hindsight, the fact of their simultaneous occurrence renders us far less confident of our ability to anticipate the future. This loss of confidence—not just by the banks, but by the entire international financial system—may be the single greatest obstacle to reaching a solution.

In 1979, a major political/military event, the start of the Iran-Iraq war, was a surprise. The resulting withdrawal of oil from export markets caused a far greater price increase than occurred in 1973 and 1974. The negative impact on the external accounts of the non-oil developing countries also was greater.

But the Iran-Iraq war was only the first of a series of extraordinary events that produced today's debt problem. During the entire post-World War II period up until that point, the economic policies of the industrial countries had focused unswervingly on the twin targets of economic growth and full employment. Price stability and a sound balance of payments were also policy targets, but when conflicts arose among these four goals because of difficulties in achieving all simultaneously, employment and growth always were given priority.

After the second round of oil price increases, however, an unprecedented shift in economic policy objectives in industrial nations occurred. The decision was made in these countries to follow structural adjustment policies that implicitly assumed the prolonged, if not permanent, presence of sharply higher energy prices. In Western Europe, policies designed to reduce the relative size of physical deficits produced three years of economic stagnation, accompanied by an increase in unemployment to postwar record levels, which still persist. In West Germany, for example, the unemployment rate had been a fraction of 1 percent during most of the postwar period prior to the oil shocks. But after 1980, German unemployment soared. After more than three years of economic recovery, it is still close to 10 percent. In the United Kingdom, the unemployment rate today is around 14 percent, up from a level of 2 or 3 percent in the postwar period. In the United States, a shift in economic policies designed to reduce soaring rates of inflation and prop a weak and declining dollar required a rise in interest rates, thereby taking the prime rate to a record average level. In 1981, the U.S. prime rate was close to 19 percent, almost twice the level of the previous average high, in 1974, of a little more than 10.5 percent. Today, at 9 percent, the rate remains greater than the average for the last half of the 1970s, which by historical standards was itself a period of extraordinarily high interest rates.

The result was the global recession of 1980-1982, the longest and deepest recession since the Great Depression. The effect on the developing country borrowers has been devastating. Most of their external debt is denominated in U.S. dollars; much of that was borrowed at floating rates. The roller-coaster rise in U.S. interest rates has resulted in increases in total debt service payments far greater than anything prior experience could have led either the borrowing countries or their creditors to expect.

But more than that, the borrowing countries have been exposed to a double-edged sword. As their debt service requirements were soaring, the recession produced a steep plunge in commodity prices, the dollar began to appreciate, and there were three consecutive years of decline in world trade—also a new and unenviable record for the postwar period. Massive increases in debt service requirements, occurring simultaneously with the precipitous decline in exports and resulting foreign exchange earnings, resulted in the debt crisis with which we now are dealing.

The Effect on the Banks

But what was the effect on the banks? Logically, the banks have tried to reduce their vulnerability, but the unintended result might well be to put the large volume of already outstanding bank loans in deeper jeopardy. The current reluctance on the part of the banks to engage in more voluntary lending to debtor countries may well have a result contrary to its goal.

Substantial losses have been incurred, principally in the private sector but also, in some cases, in the public sector. Many banks also have sold claims on the developing countries at varying discounts to nonbank investors. These two factors, which may total at least $4 billion, are certainly negative impacts.

There is another aspect to the opportunity costs incurred by the banks as a result of developing country debt problems. Even without addressing the question of prospective losses, the large volume of long-term loans now are earning less than they would in alternative uses. This, of course, is diminishing the current and future profits of the banks.

Beyond these opportunity costs, developing country debt problems have resulted in an erosion of public confidence in the future profitability of the banks. This loss of confidence is not caused by *actual* losses—in contrast to a factual record of losses for U.S. banks from domestic energy and agricultural loans; rather, the concern about the banks' developing country exposure is about *potential* losses. The prices of bank stocks have not approached the earnings multiples achieved by the stocks of corporations and more investor-favored industries. Consequently, the cost of raising equity capital for the banks has been high.

Banking regulations stipulate a direct relationship between the capital of a bank and its lending activities. Of even greater importance now, bank regulators have mandated higher capital requirements in general and are proposing other changes that would require relatively higher capital requirements for loans to developing countries than for loans to industrial countries.

The practical effect of higher capital requirements and a high cost of raising equity capital has been to curtail bank lending activities and profits. Regulators, on the other hand, would argue that their actions have provided greater protection to bank depositors and shareholders.

It is true, of course, that a bank's ultimate cushion against loan losses is its capital. But capital requirements far in excess of actual needs result in reduced profits per share, lower stock prices, and even higher costs for new capital. It is not difficult to see that banks and their customers can get caught in a vicious cycle that would lead to lower lending for all types of borrowers and activities, with consequent detrimental effects for general economic performance.

The U.S. economy would be affected seriously. No activity would be immune to an across-the-board pullback in lending by the banks. Every industry in the United States, from real estate to microchips, would suffer from lack of sufficient funds or higher pricing for the limited funds that are available.

It is ironic that bank regulators are calling for increasing capital requirements for developing country loans at the same time that the Baker Plan is calling upon the banks to increase their lending to these countries. Increasing the cost of undertaking these activities, which already have imposed higher costs on the banks, hardly can be called positive reinforcement. The new tax law also will reduce loan loss provisions, which are part of banks' capital. This, too, seems counterproductive. The 1986 tax law eliminates tax credits for the banking system, which would increase the cost of lending vis-à-vis any other nation's bank in the world, leaving U.S. banks at a very significant competitive disadvantage.

Some Positive Results

But the impact of developing country debt problems on the credit of banks has not been all bad. The Baker Plan, for example, introduces a fundamentally new element into the international financial system and its dealings with the developing countries. Instead of a new set of constraints, the plan has established a mechanism for coordination between official and commercial lenders and the borrowing countries. Such a mechanism has been needed badly. It is not an answer to all the problems; no single answer exists. But this initiative represents an important development, which should have positive effects long after the current problems are resolved.

In conclusion, I am heartened by current general economic trends. Many of the events identified as the root causes of the financial distress in the developing countries have been reversed. Interest rates have fallen sharply from their peaks and will decline further. This will have a positive effect on the developing world not just in terms of lowering debt service, but also by permitting more rapid growth in the industrial countries. Falling oil prices and interest rates unquestionably will prolong the upswing in the world economy. The rapid decline of the dollar also will lead to strong growth in world trade and should provide some badly needed support for world commodity prices in the near future.

Falling oil prices do present serious problems for countries such as Mexico, Indonesia, Nigeria, and Venezuela. However, an analysis of the long-term impact on the aggregate external financing requirements of the developing world shows a net positive effect.

There are still serious problems. The most serious of all, perhaps, is the lack of confidence shown by the citizens of developing countries in their own countries' futures. Such self-doubt leads to massive capital outflows and results, indirectly, in higher borrowing requirements. The borrowers themselves must resolve this urgent problem. It is not an exaggeration to note that in some major borrowing countries, new funds provided by the commercial banks in 1987 will be matched by capital flight.

To reverse the capital flight trend, consistent and realistic exchange rate policies must be followed. Recognizing that most investors have similar incentives, developing countries must realize that until domestic savings in the debtor nations have grown and are channeled into domestic investment, foreign investment simply will not enter.

The banking community will put up new money. We, too, want to see the light at the end of the tunnel. Considering the magnitude and nature of the problems that already have been faced, I remain optimistic that, given time, solutions will be found. It is in everyone's self-interest to help find them.

Comments and Discussion on Part One

The first panel discussion was moderated by former Senator Howard Baker and former President Jimmy Carter and included symposium participants Jésus Silva-Herzog, Terence C. Canavan, and Eduardo Wiesner. Questions also were accepted from the floor.

Capital Flight

Howard Baker: Approximately $100 billion in capital from Latin American countries is invested in Europe, the United States, Canada, and elsewhere. Obviously, if a portion of that money could be repatriated not only to Mexico but to other countries of this hemisphere, it would improve Latin America's ability to solve its own problems. What, if any, proposals can you think of that might be undertaken by the countries of the western hemisphere to encourage the reinvestment of these funds in Latin America?

Jésus Silva-Herzog: This question is in the minds of almost everybody in recent times. But I wonder why capital flight was only "discovered" about six months ago. There is no question that the return of capital to Latin America would be positive. There is also no question that the only way to accomplish this objective is to achieve sound and stable growth patterns. We need to demonstrate the possibility that our economies can grow. Banks could help by not trying to attract that capital, but, of course, we live in a free market system. But my conclusion is that it would be very difficult through any administrative or other kind of measures to have that process reversed.

Many of the figures used to show the magnitude of capital flight are without foundation. It has been said, for instance, that from 1982 to 1985 Mexico has had a capital flight of more than $14 billion. Of course, that elicits an unfavorable reaction. Why should we lend more to Mexico when Mexico is not able to maintain the confidence of its own nationals? There are only three legitimate sources for estimating capital flight: the IMF, the Bank for International Settlements, and the U.S. Treasury Department. Among those three sources, the figure of $14 billion is about right—but it is the *balance,* not the *flow,* during the past three years. The flow, according to these figures, is about $3 billion in the last three years.

In recent months, with respect to Mexico, the process has been reversed because of a number of stringent credit and monetary measures. We have reduced the liquidity within the Mexican economy, and this action has forced both national and foreign companies located in Mexico to bring money back into the country for working capital or investment progress.

However, in the long term, the only way to reverse capital flight is to regain investor confidence, and such confidence is closely linked to an improvement in the economic conditions and in the economic and social prospects of the country.

Will Banks Cooperate?

Jimmy Carter: Chemical Bank, one of the largest lenders of international funds in the private sector of our nation, made practically no loans to Latin America in 1985. One of the key provisions of the Baker Plan is to have the commercial banks increase their loans rather than stop or reduce them. If the commercial banks choose not to increase their present level of lending to the developing nations that are already heavily in debt, and if the developing nations on the other hand do not open up their borders for outside investment, then where do we go from here?

In 1985, countries such as Venezuela, which was paying both the interest and something on the principal, could no longer do so. Now those who have been barely paying the interest—by borrowing money to pay it—may not be able to do that. So if the Baker Plan is ineffective, what is the next step?

Eduardo Wiesner: One of the premises of the Baker Initiative is that there should be a continuing flow of financial resources from the commercial banks to those countries that adopt policies to build a more sound basis for growth. What happens if the banks do not increase their exposure to moderate levels, for example, of 3 to 7 percent—which would still be less than one-half of what they were from 1975 to 1981? The main point for the banks is, how do you protect your assets? How do you protect your claims on the debt of countries? Should the banks recognize that new loans are a way to protect those assets? I do not know.

Terence C. Canavan: The Baker Plan is an extremely good initiative, and more than 99 percent of the banks by dollar volume involved in developing country lending now have endorsed it, indicating that they will provide funding when and if the plan goes forward. But I think most countries are reluctant to be the first to be identified with the Baker Plan, as that will mean fourteen other countries will be looking over its shoulders offering advice on negotiations. No negotiator wants that. Nevertheless, we will end up with the Baker Plan in a number of countries without realizing that is what happened. It will happen gradually.

Will Debt Worsen If the Baker Plan Succeeds?

Howard Baker: Even though the Baker Plan may produce a significant palliative for current problems, might it not complicate the problem by adding to the total volume of debt in the future? An article in *Fortune* magazine recently suggested that the debt will never be repaid, and there is nothing left to do except to let the banks eat it.

Terence C. Canavan: I agree totally with the analysis in the *Fortune* article. Not only will the debt never be repaid; it will become larger, although at a reduced rate. But the U.S. government's debt also will not be paid, nor will the AT&T debt.

Baker Plan and Alternatives

Jimmy Carter: At the moment, the Baker Plan seems to be the only one, and there is almost no thought given to an alternative approach. Are there any changes that must be made by creditor nations? Can the debtor nations service the debt if the funding is not approved?

Eduardo Wiesner: Inevitably, almost everyone will conclude that a solution to the debt problem needs three fundamental ingredients: (1) policy changes on the side of the indebted countries; (2) adequate financial flows, not only from the commercial banks but from those of the official governments and from all sources of financing that complement the policy changes; and (3) an auspicious economic ecology for the world. The Baker Plan assembles these three parts into one package.

The international community previously has focused on external adjustment, but now we must look at the domestic dimension, which is how to obtain growth. The Baker Initiative suggests that the only way to stimulate growth is by increasing savings and investment. Is there any country that has been able to grow without investing? No.

So what the Baker Initiative suggests is that we look at the adjustment effort, but continued adjustment cannot produce a long-term solution. The positive aspect of the Baker Initiative is that it addresses the long-term issue of durable growth.

Structural Changes

Jésus Silva-Herzog: There is still going to be a need for additional foreign savings in order to complement the domestic effort. Therefore, the debt will continue to grow. We have to increase the capacity to service and pay that debt, and that can be achieved only through more dynamic economic growth within the country, essentially by increasing exports. The only way the indebted countries can face the challenge successfully is to become more competitive, more efficient, and more able to export. Of course, Mexico is making every effort to increase exports and to foster interregional trade. The only way to grow out of the debt problem is to export more, yet the industrialized nations seem to be limiting such opportunities.

In most of our countries, there must be many changes in economic policy, but with less capital, we have fewer options. Long before the Baker Initiative, we knew of the need to save and invest. Most of the Latin American countries—Brazil, Argentina, and Mexico—have begun making structural changes since the debt crisis. Most countries have cut the public sector deficit by half. We know we have to introduce changes in many aspects of our economic policies.

Government Coordination of Bank Loans

Howard Baker: Should there be more coordination between governments and banks on commercial loans abroad?

Terence C. Canavan: The private sector should deal with its business, whether that business is with the private sector or with governments. Any umbrella group that put political considerations rather than economic considerations in the forefront would be less efficient than any other system. I would worry a lot about how an alternative system would be used in the future. If I represented a government—whether in Latin America, Asia, or Africa—I would worry even more.

Jésus Silva-Herzog: We should look for a greater level of coordination between multilateral institutions and commercial banks. We are making substantial progress in that respect. Other kinds of coordination would be counterproductive.

We have to realize that much of the very heavy borrowing and lending that took place in the 1970s and early 1980s occurred because everyone was wrong about the future of the oil markets. Seventy-five percent of the Mexican debt was obtained when the price of oil was $32 a barrel. Almost everyone made a bad judgment.

Capital and Development

Eduardo Wiesner: From 1973 or 1974 until 1980 and 1981, it was thought that if countries were given financial resources, they would develop. It was thought that if those resources came from the private sector, then there was no risk to the public or to the private sector or to the indebted countries. History has proven that wrong.

Something else remarkable happened during that period—domestic savings as a percentage of GNP in most Latin American countries declined. The seeds of a crisis were sown when domestic savings declined at the very moment that gigantic financial flows were arriving to the same countries.

How did we get into this? Because it was thought that development was the result of financing. Of course, development is much more complex. Constructing the basis for sustainable growth will be a tremendous task for several generations. However, if the wrong policies led to this crisis, the right policies will get us out.

Changing FDIC Rules

Question: The Federal Deposit Insurance Corporation (FDIC) has relaxed certain requirements on energy-related loans or agricultural loans in the Midwest and Southwest. Can or should the FDIC take similar action on foreign loans? Would that help?

Terence C. Canavan: I doubt whether the FDIC would apply its new regulation to international banking. What impact would it have? The commercial banks have about 65 to 70 percent of the debt. The rest is held by governments and others. Of the bank debt, U.S. banks hold about 36 to 38 percent. So about 63 percent in commercial bank debt does not belong to any U.S. bank. It belongs to the Japanese, the Germans, the Swiss, the English, and so on. A change by the FDIC could have an impact on banks' financial statements, but that really would not give us any advantage. There are advantages in the other banking systems—the ability to create reserves on a nontax basis, for example—that the U.S. banking system does not have, so we would continue to be at a disadvantage, particularly with the passage of the new tax law.

Loans and Leverage

Question: If it were necessary to renew Latin American loans at less than the prime rate, should there be a relaxation of the classification of those loans by banking regulatory authorities?

Terence C. Canavan: If you want to judge the risk of these portfolios right now, we are dealing at less than market. Nevertheless, when you start going less than costs, using current regulations, these loans immediately become nonperforming assets, with all that entails as far as capital requirements and such.

Banks around the world do not want to relinquish authority, or leverage, by capitalizing debt—because we end up with the same debt at the end of the day. We want to retain both loans and leverage, saying "This money is yours, if you meet your side of the bargain." The Latin American side of the bargain is to make the necessary structural reforms and policy changes. If we start capitalizing and the debtor countries start saying, "We will just pay 4 percent this year instead of 7," I think we lose a little bit of control. We no longer have the leverage to insist that the countries do their share on the structural side.

U.S. Deficits

Question: Is not the greatest imbalance really in terms of the fiscal policy of the United States? Why blame the entire debt problem on the Latin American countries?

Eduardo Wiesner: I think the question is well posed and valid. If we agree that the indebted countries must change their domestic policies, what about the creditor countries?

part two

Long-Term Solutions

chapter seven

Resolving The Debt Crisis: A U.S. Perspective

Bill Bradley

Solving the debt crisis is a formidable challenge. Furthermore, it is a crisis for *all* Americans, not just for those living south of the United States. The United States should be vitally interested in Latin American economic growth and political stability. Threats to Latin peace and prosperity jeopardize collective security in the Americas and can be effectively contained only by collective action.

A Partnership for Growth

North, Central, and South Americans share a common interest in the success of Latin democracies. But democracy cannot take root and flourish without the tangible promise of a better life, and that means economic growth. Poverty must be attacked. Hopes must be fulfilled. Realizing this dream of a better life for our American community will take more than a formula for managing debt. It requires a partnership between our two regions, built upon mutual respect, democratic values, and a determination to assure adequate food, health care, and education as well as human rights and personal freedom. It is that partnership for growth that I want to propose.

Before I describe a plan for debt, let me explain the stakes that the United States has in making this partnership work. The stakes can be reduced to two issues: jobs in the United States and democracy in Latin America.

U.S. Jobs

The simple truth is that the unacknowledged victims of the debt crisis are U.S. workers. It is true, of course, that Latin countries have taken draconian austerity measures to swell their exports and shrink their imports so they could service their debt, and they have made a Herculean effort. But let us not forget what their success has meant for U.S. workers: the loss of more than 1 million jobs. The price the United States has paid for Latin America's ability to meet its new debt schedules has been the collapse of Latin markets for U.S. products.

At the same time, Latins exported goods to the United States instead of consuming them at home. That helped their balance of payments, but it reduced their standard of living, because virtually every dollar Latin Americans have earned from their exports has been spent on debt service. There have been devastating results for their growth and for U.S. trade:

- In 1983, the United States lost one-third of its exports to Latin America.
- In the two-year period from 1981 to 1983, exports of U.S. machinery fell by 38 percent; steel and motor vehicles fell by 50 percent; construction equipment dropped by almost 80 percent; and agricultural machinery was cut by more than 85 percent.
- Between 1981 and 1985, 80 percent of the markets lost by U.S. soybean growers were attributable to an Argentine export drive required by its creditors.
- In the period from 1983 to 1986, the debt crisis has added half a percentage point to U.S. unemployment each year and billions to the budget deficit.
- Between 1981 and 1984, the annual U.S. trade deficit with Latin America increased by $23 billion, compared with an $18 billion increase in the U.S. trade deficit with Japan and an estimated $15 to $20 billion in unfair trade practices worldwide—the two factors, Japan and unfair trade, that usually get blamed for the huge trade deficit in the United States.

U.S. workers and farmers have lost jobs and markets while banks have continued to profit from Latin American loans. The economic security of millions of Americans requires a better deal.

Democracy in Latin America

But the U.S. partnership with its Latin neighbors embraces more than the job security of U.S. workers. We U.S. citizens also care about the consolidation of democracy in Latin America, and we recognize that democracy is premised on growth. Yet, poverty is tightening its grip on Central and South America as resources drain from the region. Nor is all of this draining due to debt repayments. In the last three years, capital flight has siphoned off more than $30 billion—funds that should have been invested in fueling Latin

American growth. Some bankers claim that as much as fifty cents on every dollar of new loans to a country like Mexico will find its way into Miami real estate or Swiss bank accounts. Any effective policy to manage these countries' debts will have to deal with this problem. Success in doing so will depend not only on sound economic policies but also on political will.

Sadly, capital flight, together with Latin America's efforts to stay current on debt payments, has created a recession in most Latin countries by depriving them of investment they need to keep growing. Living standards have fallen as a direct result of austerity conditions imposed by foreign lenders. From their peaks in 1980 through 1985, real standards of living fell 8 percent in Mexico, 14 percent in Peru, 17 percent in Argentina, and 19 percent in Venezuela. In Mexico, non-oil public investment is at the 1964 level, even though the population has increased by 30 million people. There is an increasingly volatile political climate in Mexico, in which plummeting living standards easily can become an issue custom-made for demagogues. The Peronists in Argentina are trying to make President Alfonsín pay for his pragmatic stand toward debt repayment. Even President García of Peru is finding that his hardline position on debt has not isolated him from terrorist attacks. Looking beyond the impact of the debt crisis, we must worry about the future of democracy throughout the region.

Unless we help present leaders counter poverty successfully, we should not be surprised if their successors choose a noncapitalist model to deal with poverty. We cannot complain when their present good will turns into hostility toward the United States. The U.S. debt policy hurts its neighbors to the south today and makes political turmoil more probable tomorrow.

The Baker Plan: A Blueprint with Flaws

As a partner in the inter-American community, the united States can no longer allow the debt crisis to foreclose Latin America's chances for democracy and growth, and mortgage its future to debt service. Some might say that the Reagan administration's proposal, the Baker Plan, is a way to avert so bleak an outcome. But that is not so.

The Baker Plan is first and foremost an admission on the part of the U.S. government that the approach it had been pursuing had reached a dead end. The plan is a repudiation of the international economic policy of Reagan's first five years—and, as a blueprint for the future it is, on the one hand, too ambitious in calling for drastic internal changes from Latin debtor countries and, on the other, not ambitious enough in showing debtors and creditors alike a way out of the debt crisis while putting a premium on the well-being of the Latin American people.

The Baker Plan rests on the traditional assumption that the debtor countries, left to their own devices, cannot be trusted to implement "sound" economic policies. Hence, these policies must be imposed from abroad as a condition of getting new money from banks—a kind of supply-side imperialism. The conditions insisted upon by the Reagan administration are rooted in strong ideological bias—run the economy through a wringer; shrink the public sector; put people out of work; cut wages; cut public services; cut imports; "privatize"; puncture the rising expectations of the middle class; relegate millions of people to a future of poverty and despair—so long as the banks get paid. But the plan offers no clarity about the relation between new commercial lending and new multilateral lending. The assumption behind the Baker Plan is that the debt problem is primarily economic, best handled by bankers, not by politicians held accountable to voters. This point of view is profoundly antidemocratic.

In addition, the Reagan administration has been remiss in focusing unduly on the military conflict in Central America. The $100 million in aid to contras would barely cover the cost of one single day's debt service for that region. It is high time the administration acknowledged that political turmoil is a product of economic stagnation and that a failure to assist economic development can change all too easily into strategic losses for the United States. It will not be enough to have aided the contras if Mexico is engulfed in political chaos because the U.S. attached less value to Mexican prosperity than to the convenience of foreign bankers. Yet were Mexico to collapse, the controversy about Nicaragua would be only a sideshow. U.S. leadership in Latin America would become a fiction.

An Alternative Approach

I am proposing an approach that recognizes that the debt issue offers the political opportunity of a generation. This alternative approach substitutes partnership for conditionality and replaces austerity with growth as the central concepts of a long-term solution to the debt problem. The approach also breaks the standoff between the banks, debtors, and multilateral agencies that threatens to bog down debt management and makes Latin American initiative, not supply-side dogmatism, the basis of a strategy for sustainable growth. This proposal says to Latin America that now is the time to take your place as a partner in pursuit of commonly shared democratic values, of more efficient economies, of improved standards of living, and of a deeper cultural understanding of our two distinct traditions.

Unlike the Baker Plan, the proposal I am suggesting recognizes that debt management can play only a secondary role in reviving Latin economies. It is necessary but not sufficient. Ultimately it is up to the Latin governments to make the basic changes needed to restore confidence, stem capital flight, encourage investment, and let markets work. That is why my approach explicitly asks debtor countries to come forward with specific initiatives to rekindle growth and nurture democratic institutions in exchange for creditors' easing of the debt burden.

That is why my proposal emphasizes debt relief more than new commercial loans. In the long run, the U.S. national interest, the interests of the inter-American community, and the stability of the international financial system all depend on making the debt burden bearable. New lending is becoming politically intolerable in Latin America and is threatening the stability of money center banks, which continue to have inadequate capital to cover new Latin American exposure. Enormous interest/export ratios of close to 50 percent are discouraging new investment in Latin America. Yet the Baker Plan misguidedly calls for still more new loans, not less.

In brief, here is what I propose. The core of my proposal is a seven-member council that will coordinate the actions of commercial creditors, creditor governments, and multilateral lending agencies. This coordinating council will evaluate debtor country growth proposals and offer a package of debt relief options that is appropriate to a specific plan. The council will include one representative of the U.S. government and two representatives of the European Economic Community, Canada, and Japan; three representatives of commercial creditors; and the president of the World Bank, for a total membership of seven. Every major class of creditors is represented, and banks get equal representation with governments. At the same time, the council remains small enough to be manageable.

The council's first function will be to invite proposals for growth from those debtor countries that the members agree need debt relief. Second, the council will evaluate the proposals and issue general recommendations for debt relief. In making its evaluations, the council shall be guided by six principles. The first three principles reflect political values; the remaining three, economic realities.

First, the debtor growth plan should enjoy broad-based domestic support. Deals between debtor governments and creditor banks that impose harsh costs of adjustment on the rank and file in an indebted country are no better than deals that pay off banks while forcing U.S. workers out of their jobs. Second, the plan should rely on democratic processes. Specifically, growth plans should be subjected to the challenges of a competitive political system, and their survival should reflect some form of broad political consensus. Third, the plans should be immune from corrupt administration. Debt relief should not line the pockets of a corrupt elite.

Economic principles governing the council's debt proposals should emphasize growth over austerity as well as the development of internal strengths over export promotion and import substitution. Accordingly, the fourth criterion of any debt relief plan should be its ability to promote stable, noninflationary growth. Because growth is sporadic even in the most developed countries, however, the fifth criterion is also economic: the ability of the plan to induce internal savings. Without internal savings, a country can never be self-reliant. The sixth criterion, particularly relevant for Mexico and Venezuela, should be the ability of the plan to stem capital flight. The nation's domestic investors must vote with their savings if foreign creditors are to participate in new development.

The council also will focus on the social programs and political institutions that are essential in restoring or maintaining citizen confidence in government. This is critical because without that confidence, people will not invest their capital and talent in their nation's future, but rather, those resources will be shipped abroad, depriving the country of necessary investment for growth.

A panel of economic and financial experts will assist the coordinating council by providing objective evaluations of the debtor country proposals. As I now envision it, this technical panel will consist of five members—one from the Inter-American Development Bank, one from the International Monetary Fund, and three outside experts chosen by the Group of Five ministers, the Cartagena steering group, and the commercial creditors. Among the kinds of relief the council could recommend are temporary interest rate relief, relief on official loans, and loans from the World Bank for projects that can be completed quickly.

Let me be more specific. Creditors should offer debt and interest rate relief and increased multilateral aid in exchange for debtor reforms that will generate growth. As a target for the total value of annual debt relief packages that would be offered to eligible countries, I suggest:

- 3 points of interest rate relief for one year on all outstanding commercial and bilateral loans to eligible countries
- 3 percent write-down and forgiveness of principal on all outstanding commercial and bilateral loans to eligible countries
- $3 billion of new multilateral project and structural adjustment loans for eligible countries

These relief packages should be carefully tailored to the needs and commitments of each country. The actual value and mix of each yearly trade/debt relief package should depend on the uses that each debtor has made of a previous year's package. The relief should vary from year to year and from country to country, depending on results. Although reforms coming from within will differ from country to country, they generally should liberalize trade, reverse capital flight, increase internal investment, promote economic growth, and enjoy broad internal political support.

Making debt relief work for U.S. creditors also will require a regulatory review board to consider how bank regulations and interpretations of tax and accounting rules must be changed or clarified to allow debt restructuring decisions. In the final analysis, the kind of coordination I am proposing is necessary to avoid having tax and accounting habits forestall a solution to the growth crisis.

An Opportunity for Leadership, An Opportunity for Growth

I recognize that the mechanism I am suggesting cannot solve the debt crisis by itself. It will be only as effective as the policies it implements. Its principal advantage is that it places a premium on nurturing growth in debt-burdened nations—growth that reaches the people and stimulates democracy. To this end, the council encourages inter-American cooperation and a forum for working problems out.

After World War II, the United States stepped boldly into the role of international economic leader and pathbreaker. Recognizing the need to rebuild Europe, the United States, through the Marshall Plan, challenged Europe to propose plans for growth that could be supplemented with U.S. aid. Today, Latin America needs rebuilding. It needs to propose plans for growth that will be supplemented with debt relief and, in Central America, with direct economic aid. Latin America needs to be able to hold its head high, confident that it can better the lives of its citizens, accepting responsibility for its future and blaming no one for its past.

Once again, the United States has the opportunity to lead effectively. Let us in the United States not wait for wars or earthquakes to take bold initiatives for our common good. We should challenge Latin America to adopt long-term plans for growth, to back them with commitments, and to propose realistic roles for its creditors. But, in order to get respect, the United States must give it. We must recognize that Latin America might choose differently than we on some domestic issues, and yet we must remain confident that independence based on increasing prosperity, democratic values, and discipline cannot be anything but reassuring.

The inter-American community has demonstrated its belief that debt should be repaid. My proposal is a way to get creditors and debtors working together toward that end. At the same time, it strengthens the bonds between our different cultural traditions and recognizes that we all, ultimately, want the same things for our citizens: peace, prosperity, and freedom.

chapter eight

Resolving the Debt Crisis: A Latin American Perspective

Manuel Azúrua

The external debt of the Latin American countries has become, in the last few years, one of the fundamental issues defining the present and future of inter-American relations. This problem cannot be understood solely in terms of its economic and financial dimensions; it has become the center of a complex universe that affects the political, diplomatic, social, and cultural relations between the countries of Latin America and the industrialized countries, especially those in the western hemisphere. The Latin American external debt already exceeds $368 billion, and more than one-third of that amount is owed to financial institutions in the United States and Canada. Much is at stake, including the economic viability of our countries, the future of the international financial system, and the evolution of the relationships between the different participants in that system. Because of the importance of these problems, the need for a definitive solution is imperative.

How the Debt Crisis Began

The Latin America debtor countries have not evaded their responsibility in this crisis. The normal transfer of financial resources from the more developed countries, with low interest rates and long terms, had complemented the insufficient domestic savings of our economies. However, at the end of the 1970s, bank loans exceeded the absorptive capacity of our development program. External credit was preferred as a source of financing investment projects, not all of them justifiable. In some cases, loans were used to finance nonproductive government expenditures for which there was no source of domestic financing. The excess of liquidity generated in the international credit markets and the extraordinary dynamism of the international financial institutions allowed for the transfer of large amounts of resources to the developing economies—beyond what was prudent.

The instability of international money markets and the upsurge of inflation, which gave rise to high interest rates, both nominal and real, reduced the term of new credits and transformed the underlying structural problems into a crisis of large proportions. In the beginning of the crisis, we were reluctant to comprehend its full implications; some even ignored it. The easy flow of new credits permitted a temporary solution of the liquidity problem at the expense of our future development. However, the impossibility of meeting all the external debt obligations became clear in 1982, in what has come to be known as the "debt crisis."

The Evolution of the Problem

Recently, we have begun to see an evolution. We have moved from short-term, emergency solutions at the start of the crisis to demonstrations of concern for the debt problem's long-term implications. We now see the need for definitive solutions. The domestic adjustment programs of the Latin American economies have allowed the fulfillment of financial obligations more or less within the terms established in the different restructuring agreements. However, this has been at the expense of a very deep economic recession in the entire region, caused by a drastic curtailment of imports and the contraction of private and public investment. The external environment has made the adjustments more difficult and the financial and commercial crisis more severe.

In fact, Latin America has become a net *exporter* of capital. During the period from 1982 through 1985, the transfer of resources to the creditor countries reached $106 billion. Meanwhile, the prices of our export products declined significantly; the terms of trade deteriorated by 16.5 percent between 1981 and the end of 1985. At the same time, the slowdown of international trade has precluded the recovery of export volumes, while the decline in prices diminished the level of export income.

Although nominal interest rates have declined, their real values remain at historically high levels. Moreover, the drastic fall in oil prices exacerbates the deterioration of the economies of countries such as Mexico, Ecuador, and Venezuela because oil is their main source of external income. This situation has had a negative effect on the financial and economic crisis of Latin America.

Where Do We Go from Here?

Certainly, the financial terms that have been agreed upon in the most recent restructuring agreements are somewhat more favorable to the debtor countries than previous arrangements. But we all must recognize that the definitive solution to this debt crisis can be accomplished only when our countries overcome the current recession and the international economy is strengthened.

An effective program, however, cannot be limited to solutions based solely on increases in the flow of funds to debtor countries. In order for a program to address the debt problem successfully, it should include the following points:

- Domestic policies should be oriented to achieve noninflationary, sustained economic growth in *all* countries, industrialized and developing.
- There should be changes in the trade policies of the industrialized countries to eliminate protectionist practices and reduce the external disequilibrium of the main developed economies.
- There should be changes in the norms that govern international financial operations. Coordination of monetary and exchange rate policies should be improved among the main central banks—the fundamental actors in the international financial system—so as to reduce interest rates substantially in the shortest possible time.
- The compensatory financing mechanisms of international financial institutions should be strengthened to compensate for the deterioration of the terms of trade and protect against sudden increases in interest rates and long-term refinancing of interest costs.
- There should be substantial increases in the financing resources of the multilateral institutions and reforms that allow the rapid disbursement of loans granted by these institutions. This should be done in order to guarantee the maximum profitability and effectiveness of the financed programs, without affecting the inalienable sovereign right of the recipient countries to determine and decide their own policies and priorities for economic and social development.
- Clearer economic policies and rules are needed to stimulate the return and reinvestment of capital placed abroad by nationals from the debtor countries.

Leadership and Solidarity

The implementation of a program like the one outlined here requires difficult and risky decisions. The need to act fast is self-evident. Our long-term economic development and the viability of democracy as a political system in Latin American countries are at stake. At other times in history, our more developed neighbors have had the opportunity to play leading roles in moments of crisis in other parts of the world.

The United States and Canada have, today, the historic opportunity to exercise leadership and promote intercontinental solidarity in economic relations and to accelerate the reforms that will permit the implementation of this program. If they do so, they could overcome the problems we face today and restore a vigorous and sustained process of economic growth that could be conducive to the consolidation of the democratic system of the continent.

chapter nine

The View of the Reagan Administration: Toward Stronger World Growth

David C. Mulford

The international debt crisis continues to pose one of the greatest challenges for the world economy and financial system since the Great Depression. As with all megaproblems confronting world governments, the debt crisis has that element of monolithic insolubility that brings out our worst frustrations. Like an elephant, it is easy to see, hard to get your arms firmly around, and very unproductive to face the entire bulk head on.

By the end of 1985, the external debt of the developing nations had grown to more than $900 billion—more than $200 billion higher than at the onset of the debt crisis in early 1982 and nearly triple the debt in 1977. Forty percent of this debt is in Latin America; about $420 billion is owed to the private commercial banks, with $120 billion of that sum owed to U.S. commercial banks. Interest charges alone on these vast sums presently amount to $75 billion a year, and total debt service prior to reschedulings amounts to some $140 billion annually, representing by any measure a significant share of debtors' total export earnings.

Commodity markets generally remain depressed, and per capita income in many Latin countries remains less than earlier levels. Inflation rates in Latin America are two-and-a-half times as high as they were in 1980 and investment has fallen sharply.

Managing the debt problem, let alone eventually solving it, requires two critical operating assumptions. First, we must honestly recognize that there are no easy, all-encompassing global solutions. Second, no matter how overpowering the problem appears in its totality, we must focus our efforts on solvable elements of the problem and work to expand those once they are established.

The U.S. Debt Initiative: International Context

Herein lies the importance of the U.S. debt initiative, known as the Baker Plan. It recognizes as its first and foremost element the fundamental need for growth and places the objective of increased growth at the center of the debt strategy. Perhaps in our preoccupation with balance-of-payments crises, standby programs, reschedulings, and new bank financing we have not kept two very simple facts firmly in our minds.

- First, without growth there can be no solution to the debt problem. Countries will never be able to repay any portion of the debt they are carrying unless they can accumulate resources—and export earnings—at a faster pace than they are accumulating debt.
- Second, without economic reform, no amount of money—whether derived from external borrowing, financial aid, or inflationary domestic pump-priming—will produce sustained growth.

One needs only to observe the pernicious problem of capital flight, which in recent years has been equivalent to virtually all new bank lending to Latin America, to see the futility of throwing more money at the problem. Credible reform by the debtor nations will improve their growth prospects, but economic adjustment and growth must be financed. The other two elements of the debt initiative provide for the sources of this finance: new net lending by commercial banks and enhanced flows from the international financial institutions. These three mutually reinforcing elements form the working heart of the debt strategy.

It is important to underline the fact that the debt initiative does not operate in a vacuum nor in isolation from other critical economic issues. Indeed, the debt initiative was launched by Secretary Baker shortly after the broad-based initiative taken by the Group of Five industrial nations at their meeting September 22, 1985, in New York. The Plaza agreement has resulted in a major change in relative exchange rates, and the five ministers also agreed that solid, low-inflation growth and open markets in the industrial countries are essential prerequisites for strong world growth.

The individual policy intentions announced by the Group of Five in their September statement focused on reducing structural impediments to growth, cutting excessive government expenditures, avoiding protectionist trade measures, and improving the investment climate as a stimulus to private sector initiative and growth. These measures are essential to consolidate and improve growth prospects within the industrial economies and will help increase the demand for debtor nations exports, while reducing both nominal and real interest rates in time—thus passing on the benefits of growth.

Changes in the global economic environment already are having a beneficial impact on prospects for future growth. The 35 percent decline in the dollar versus the yen and deutsche mark since February 1985 will help to improve the competitive environment for U.S. industry both at home and abroad. Interest rates also have declined sharply in reflection of both the U.S. commitment to Gramm-Rudman budget deficit reduction and falling oil prices. U.S. short-term rates have fallen from more than 11 percent in 1984 to 7.5 percent in April 1986, very similar to the decline in the London Interbank Offered Rate (LIBOR) during this same period. U.S. long-term interest rates have similarly declined from 13.5 percent to 9.5 percent during this period. These changes are important for U.S. businesses and for debtor nations. The major debtor countries are expected to save $7 to $8 billion in interest payments on their debt in 1986.

The dramatic reduction in oil prices is expected to give further impetus to stronger growth and lower interest rates in the industrial nations in the period ahead. This will provide indirect benefits for most developing countries in addition to direct benefits from reduced oil import costs. Thus, the difficulty experienced by oil exporters ought not to obscure the stimulus to recovery and growth that the fall in oil prices provides the global economy as a whole.

Unfinished Business

Although both the Group of Five initiative and the debt initiative are well advanced, there remains a considerable amount of unfinished business in both areas. In his 1986 State of the Union address, President Reagan called for closer economic coordination among the major trading countries and directed Treasury Secretary Baker to determine if the nations of the world should convene to discuss the role and relationship of our currencies.

Discussions on the need to improve the international monetary system have occurred in the Interim Committee of the IMF. The present flexible exchange rate system has served us well these past fifteen years in dealing with a world economy faced with multiple economic shocks. However, the system has had its weaknesses, and there is a need to reduce the kind of exchange rate variability that has characterized the system in recent years. A consensus is emerging that greater exchange market stability critically depends on achieving better convergence of favorable economic performance and compatible policies among the key currency countries.

The fundamental issue is how to encourage sovereign nations to pursue mutually consistent and reinforcing policies. The Group of Five Plaza agreement represented a major advance in economic collaboration. The Interim

Committee is considering recommendations to strengthen the IMF's ability to promote sound, consistent policies that move in the right direction. However, the United States is convinced that more can and should be done.

The response to the U.S. debt initiative from all quarters has been positive, confirming our conviction that the focus of the initiative is on target. To be sure, there are differing views on whether the amount of resources we have called for is sufficient, and many question whether the necessary reforms in the international financial institutions and the debtor nations can be accomplished. Others believe there should be greater involvement on the part of creditor governments. But our focus on the three main elements for resolving the debt problem is widely agreed by all key participants as holding the greatest hope for realistic forward momentum. What, then, needs to happen to make the strategy work?

First, the debtor nations must reform their economies so that they can grow. Although the developing nations as a whole have undertaken commendable efforts to deal with their debt problems during the past three years, these efforts have fallen short of producing lasting reform within their domestic economies and have failed to control adequately government budget deficits. Some progress has been made in reducing inflation, but in most countries inflation remains extremely high. Overvalued exchange rates, subsidies, and negative interest rates also frustrate the ability of the market to allocate resources efficiently within debtor economies. A resulting lack of confidence in the prospects for renewed domestic growth has contributed to serious capital flight.

A number of important structural reforms are needed to lay a firm foundation for strong growth and to reverse the capital flight that has plagued these economies. These include privatization of public enterprises, development of more efficient domestic capital and equity markets, growth-oriented tax reform, improvement of the environment for both domestic and foreign investment, trade liberalization, and rationalization of import regimes. I recognize that many of these touch on sensitive political issues, while their benefits may become visible only in the long term. Such reform is difficult and takes time. Moreover, it has to be financed; but to attract that finance it must be credible, with reasonable prospects for long-term success.

Second, new efforts are required by the international financial institutions. I would underscore at the outset that the IMF must continue to play its very important role in the overall debt strategy. Enhanced roles for the World Bank and the other multilateral development banks will be supplemental to the IMF's role, not a substitute for it.

We have asked the IMF to give more thought to growth-oriented policies; this is being done. But given the IMF's central mission (which is not that of a development institution) and its need to concentrate its resources on relatively short balance of payments programs, the IMF's contributions necessarily will focus primarily on macroeconomic policy, rather than on long-term structural reforms.

The World Bank's mission, on the other hand, is more strongly focused on longer-term development issues, and it already is experienced in addressing some of the types of structural problems that most debtor countries face. Most of the World Bank's new lending will be fast-disbursing sectoral and structural adjustment loans, as opposed to more traditional project loans. We believe the World Bank has ample capacity to increase such lending by some $2 billion per year from 1986 to 1989 and to concentrate that lending more heavily on the large debtors with credible reform programs. We also are prepared, if all the participants in the strategy do their part and there is a demonstrated increase in the demand for quality lending in excess of these levels, to consider a general capital increase for the World Bank.

It will be essential for the IMF and the World Bank to establish a closer working relationship. I realize this is easy to say and harder to accomplish. But the member governments of both institutions must insist that some pragmatic method of closer cooperation be developed if economic reform in the debtor nations is going to be credible enough to command additional resources from private banking institutions. Private lenders must be convinced that the long-term structural reforms that have not been emphasized sufficiently in the past actually will occur.

Third, commercial banks in virtually all the major creditor nations have now indicated their willingness to support the U.S. debt initiative and to provide net new lending to the debtor nations. If the other two parts of the strategy are implemented in a credible manner, the banks can gain only by providing additional financing that will improve the creditworthiness of their existing clients. The banks know that without growth in the debtor nations— and an improved ability to earn foreign exchange—they cannot expect to be repaid, nor, to put it bluntly, can they expect to continue receiving favorable earnings on assets of declining quality. The banks also know that growth must be financed in large part from private capital resources.

The Process Already Has Begun

When is the debt initiative going to begin?

The answer very simply is that it *has* begun. It is an ongoing process. Virtually all of the debtor countries are participating in this process, some more fully and successfully than others. There is no need for countries to formally embrace the plan. Indeed, the very word *plan* is misleading because the debt initiative does not prescribe a specific blueprint or plan for implementation in every detail by each and every debtor country. Rather, it provides a framework, or a grouping of mutually reinforcing elements, to enable cooperative action in support of the debtors' own efforts to improve their growth prospects.

Some of the larger debtors will need to take advantage of all of the elements of the strategy: an IMF program, enhanced sectoral loans from the multilateral development banks, and new money packages from the commercial banks. Mexico and Argentina already are working in this direction.

Other nations already have certain elements of the strategy in place. Their most immediate need is to take advantage of the new resources being provided by the multilateral development banks by adopting effective structural reforms. We are working with the World Bank to effect these flows in a relatively short period of time. Ecuador is perhaps the most advanced of this group of countries, but others such as Colombia, Uruguay, and the Ivory Coast also are making good progress and no doubt will unlock further resources from these institutions in the coming months.

The substantial exchange rate changes that have occurred since the Plaza agreement in September 1985 will help reduce the large trade imbalances among the major countries. However, in an effort to improve the functioning of the system, the United States needs to focus on ways to achieve greater growth in Europe and Japan, combined with continued improvements in access to Japanese markets, if we are to reduce substantially the large imbalances that will remain in the system. The U.S. success in implementing Gramm-Rudman budget deficit reductions and accomplishing tax reform also will be important. Finally, a new round of trade negotiations should give further impetus to global growth through the mutual reduction of trade barriers.

If the debtor nations also do their part in adopting growth-oriented reforms—and if they are supported in their efforts by additional lending from the international financial institutions and the commercial banks—the debt situation should be both manageable and containable in the period ahead.

chapter ten

A Three-Pronged Proposal for Alleviating the Debt Crisis

Pedro-Pablo Kuczynski

There is no standard long-term development solution to the debt problem for a very simple reason: the debt of the Latin American countries is currently equivalent on average to four times their annual export earnings. This means if the interest rate is, say, 10 percent, as much as 40 percent of export earnings must be devoted to servicing the interest. The only way out of the problem in the long run, then, is to increase exports—and that can be achieved only if economies grow, and that requires capital.

Another factor making a "solution" difficult is that a large part of what was borrowed was not reinvested in the countries themselves, but was reinvested abroad. An exact figure, of course, is impossible to obtain, but obviously if you mortgage your house and use the money to buy a Ferrari, then you have a problem—that is to some extent what has happened here.

Instead of "solving" the debt problem, we should talk about alleviating it. To do so requires contributions from all the parties involved: the borrowers, the governments, and the regulators in the lending banks' countries as well as the banks themselves and the international agencies. Clearly, alleviation of the debt problem cannot succeed if contributions are one-sided rather than multilateral.

Lastly, we cannot avoid immediate problems, which are going to require imaginative solutions because the financial gap that some countries face is very large and very uncertain. Fluctuations in oil prices alone—$14 a barrel this week, $9 the next—make long-range planning very difficult indeed.

Long-term Proposals

Although the debt crisis presents a long-term challenge, we must begin taking steps to alleviate it *now*. Let me sketch three parts of a proposal. The first requirement is capital. In 1985, Latin America had a trade surplus of about 4 percent of the GNP—twice the relative trade surplus of Japan—and, therefore, Latin America is a major factor in the U.S. trade deficit. That trade surplus is what has financed, to a very large degree, the repayment of interest, roughly 5 percent of GNP. Obviously, this situation cannot continue for very long. Fortunately, the very large levels of capital inflows of the late 1970s are not necessary, for the simple reason that much of that capital went in one door and out the other. However, some net inflow of capital is required.

Second, and equally important, policy changes are needed. The borrowing of the 1970s led to a huge inflation in the role of the state in several Latin American countries, although not in all. Mexico, Venezuela, and Peru are the three clearest cases. They were and still are oil-exporting countries; that fact, plus the borrowing, led to an enormous increase in the role of the public sector. As an average for Latin America as a whole, public sector expenditure as a percentage of the GNP increased from 28 percent in 1970 to 42 percent in 1980. This increase was faster than almost anywhere else in the world except for Sweden. As the past decade demonstrates,the management of state enterprise has in general been poor. As any private entrepreneur in Latin America can testify, the long-term result is a crowding-out effect on credit that gradually strangles the private sector. Policy changes, however, could alleviate greatly this aspect of the debt problem.[1]

The third requirement is a proper international setting. What does that mean? First, a buoyant world economy, more so than what we have had since 1982, is necessary. However, a proper setting also means favorable terms of trade—or at least not negative terms of trade. The raw materials Latin America exports to the outside world have fallen in price by about 25 percent since 1980, thereby making it difficult for countries to move forward. The volume of Latin American exports has gone up about 25 percent since 1981, but the value of exports has not changed. For the future this means that debtor countries must redirect their efforts toward manufactured products, as the Asian countries have done; otherwise, these countries will face long-term difficulties and a weak export performance.

Such a change is easier said than done. The task is enormous, both internally and also because of inevitable protectionist obstacles. But it *can* be done. Half of Brazil's exports, for example, are of manufactured or semi-manufactured products. Furthermore, the growth rate of Brazil's industrial product exports has been just as fast as those of the East Asian countries in the 1970s and 1980s.

The Legacy

Why are not the "right" policies being followed? There are a number of historical reasons that need to be understood before a plan can be developed to overcome the region's economic obstacles. The first key point is that the larger Latin American countries have had large protected domestic markets for a long time. Brazil, Argentina, and Mexico together make up nearly 75 percent of the economies of the region. These three countries have large markets, especially when compared to the East Asian countries. The situation in Buenos Aires or São Paulo is very different from that of Taipei, where the thought of 1 billion Chinese across the Straits of Quemoy is bound to spur producers to look outside for markets. The only sensible thing to do in Taiwan or Hong Kong is to export. Conversely, if you are in São Paulo or Mexico City, the natural tendency is to look inward for markets.

Second, Latin America, particularly the Spanish American countries, have had a concessionaire style of private enterprise for four centuries. During colonial rule, parcels of land as well as the rights to commerce and mining were assigned by the Spanish Crown. To a certain extent, this continues today. In the major industrial sectors in most countries, with the possible exceptions of Mexico and Brazil, there are only one or two companies in each field. These companies, understandably, are very much in favor of price controls and market sharing and a variety of arrangements that, in the end, impede competition and growth. Such companies, then, are protected, not only against the outside world, but from inside competition. This concessionaire mentality no doubt will give way gradually to a more competitive attitude, but this change will take time. Without growth and expanding markets, however, change cannot take place. Thus, the restoration of growth is not only an urgent priority in itself, but also is a precondition for reform.

Finally, there is a historic tradition of moderate savings combined with high consumption that has continued for hundreds of years, and will take time to change. Fortunately, a counter trend has begun in the last few decades—which is partly the result of the growth of a new generation of entrepreneurs and civil servants, many of them educated in the United States and elsewhere abroad. This new modern generation has a very different outlook that offers a foundation on which to build a different future.

The Challenge Ahead

From where will the capital necessary for growth come? As a goal, the net capital flows from abroad should be about 2 to 3 percent of the GNP. This is not unattainable.

Initially, capital will have to come from official sources, particularly the multinational development banks. At present the World Bank in particular has a considerable amount of cash and is thus in a position to substantially accelerate its disbursements. In the past these institutions have tended to lend primarily for specific projects, but that can and should change. One of the areas that must be emphasized in future lending by these institutions is investment in basic human services.

An unfortunate and neglected side effect of the debt problem is that the interest portion of the debt service absorbs a very large part of government resources. Seven or eight years ago, about 10 percent of the central government budgets was devoted to the service of interest; today, that figure is about 25 percent. This has led to large reductions in expenditures for health, education, and other human services. As compared with some countries in Asia, Latin America has done relatively well in the last decade in the areas of health and education. However future growth will be jeopardized without adequate support for these and other human needs. The returns on judiciously planned investment (as opposed to subsidies) in basic human services such as education can be very high.

Another obvious source of capital is from the private sector. The biggest source is the approximately $100 billion that Latin Americans have invested abroad. Large-scale foreign investment will return to Latin America only after some of the Latin American capital returns. Some expatriate capital is starting to return to Argentina and possibly Mexico. But it is very difficult to expect a U.S. company to invest money in markets that are flat, especially when its local partner is investing in Zurich or New York.

The only way this will change in the long run is through consistent economic policies. The sort of quick-fix changes in exchange rate policy (itself the main cause of past capital flight) for just a year or two is simply insufficient. Potential investors need to be persuaded that there is a long-term policy to keep a competitive exchange rate. Brazilians have not invested much of their capital abroad because a realistic exchange rate has been maintained for a long period.

Growth will become possible after internal policies change. Besides maintaining a competitive exchange rate, Latin America also needs to redefine the role of the state. When comparing the cost of adjustment in the period 1982 through 1984, it is instructive to look at the differences between public and private investment. Private investment essentially assumed the heaviest cost. With the exception of Mexico, however, public investment did *not* decline as a percentage of GNP. Commercial bank credit to the public sector continued at the same level of GNP—about 15 percent—whereas credit to the private sector was cut by about 50 percent (as a percentage of GNP in the same period).

Given these figures, the redefinition of the role of the state is fundamental. "Privatization" has tended to become a fashionable idea in Washington, but, in fact, many in the middle class in Latin America are strongly in favor of it. This does not require either an all-encompassing plan or years of discussion. Privatization requires a few examples of successful action. In some countries, the trend toward privatization already has begun.

Can all of this be achieved? Do we have time to do it? The answer depends on the country. Aided by the decline in oil prices and interest rates and the buoyancy of its industrial exports, Brazil is doing well. The urgent priority is that of the countries facing immediate difficulties.

The debt crisis cannot be solved. But with a consistent program aimed at increasing capital inflows, changing unworkable policies, and putting the international economy on the path of sustained growth, the worst aspects of the debt crisis can be alleviated.

Notes

1. See Bela Balassa, Gerardo M. Bueno, Pedro-Pablo Kuczynski, and Mario Henrique Simonsen, *Toward Renewed Economic Growth in Latin America* (Washington, D.C.: Institute for International Economics, 1986).

chapter eleven

The Responsibilities of the Industrialized Countries and the Need to Strengthen the World Bank

C. Fred Bergsten

There are three main sets of actors in the debt crisis: the debtor countries, the industrial countries, and the private lenders. In striving for a long-term solution to the problems of the debt, each group has an important role to play, but the World Bank needs to play the crucial role of organizing the entire effort.

The Role of the Debtor Countries

The debtor countries obviously are trying to reconcile contradictory objectives. While maintaining a responsible adjustment policy based on austerity, these countries have to resume economic growth for economic, social, and political reasons. There is only one possible strategy that can reconcile those two objectives: export-led economic growth. A growth strategy will not work unless it is based on the promotion of exports. Only with that approach can debtor countries earn the necessary foreign exchange to continue servicing their debt in a reasonably stable way and, at the same time, stimulate their economies toward consistent and sustained growth.

Latin America *can* achieve export-led growth. Many other parts of the world have done it. Although the successes of the East Asian countries are the most celebrated, Turkey, for example, has achieved dramatic export-led growth since 1980. Latin Americans themselves achieved considerable success in development in the 1960s and early 1970s, and increasing exports played an important role.

The case of Brazil deserves a closer look. Brazil is one-third of Latin America in terms of people and gross national product. In 1985, Brazil's economy grew at more than 8 percent—the fastest in the world—with a trade surplus in excess of $12 billion, and the country will become energy self-sufficient by the early 1990s. Brazil now has begun to deal with its major outstanding problem, inflation, by a sweeping monetary reform, the Cruzado Plan, and is demonstrating that even in a tough economic environment, an export-led growth strategy can work. Thus, export-led growth is not only the best means for addressing the debt crisis, but also for achieving economic growth.

The Industrial Countries' Response

The industrial countries have the major responsibility to provide an international economic environment conducive to growth. It is no accident that the debt crisis began in 1982 when the industrial countries were experiencing the deepest recession since the 1930s. It is likewise no surprise that in 1983, and particularly in 1984 when the world economy recovered strongly, that the Third World debt problem was seen as resolving itself substantially. There were enormous improvements in debt export ratios and debt service positions, and there were reductions in current account deficits of the Latin American and other debtor countries. Again, it is no surprise that with the slowdown in the world economy in 1985 and 1986, there was (and still is) increased concern about the debt crisis.

A rate of at least 3 percent growth for the industrialized countries would provide the engine of growth that could enable the debtor countries to carry out the export-led growth strategy. Interest rates must only be monitored and limited. Protectionism has to be avoided; otherwise, market access for those export efforts is impossible. The exchange rate of the dollar, which became overvalued by perhaps 40 percent at its peak in early 1985, has declined with enormous benefits for the developing countries as they try to deal with their debt problems.

However, industrial country efforts to manage the world economy effectively since 1981 have been essentially ad hoc. Even the commendable initiative in September 1985 by the U.S. Treasury Department to correct the dollar exchange rate and bring a more balanced pattern of economic growth to the world was an ad hoc response to a crisis. Similarly, the IMF has been derelict—indeed, all international institutions have been derelict—in not forging more effective, sustained coordination among the industrial countries to avoid such negative consequences as deep recessions, excessive real interest rates, misaligned currencies, and protectionist pressures. Unless better coordination is achieved, we will not have a sustained correction of the debt problem for the Third World or for the world as a whole.

The initiative that Secretary Baker of the U.S. Treasury took in September 1985 to realign the currencies is therefore more important for the debtor countries and the debt problem than the so-called Baker Plan that addresses it directly. Among other things, the currency realignment diminished protectionist pressures that were building in Congress.

But the currency realignment raises another problem. If the United States succeeds in reducing its own trade deficit by $100 to $150 billion during the next two or three years, what will be the effect on other countries? If the burden of U.S. success were to fall on the debtor developing countries, even at a level of $20 to $40 billion, the Third World would be plunged back into a more difficult phase of the debt crisis.

What is the answer to the dilemma? The United States cannot continue running trade deficits without stoking the fires of protectionism. Third World countries would be hurt by U.S. protectionism or by an improvement in the U.S. trade balance.

The answer is for the other industrial countries—Japan, Germany, and other European countries—to offset potential adverse effects of a decline in their trade surpluses (caused by a decline in the United States trade deficit) by boosting domestic demand in their economies. Japan, Germany, and other European countries have been getting *half* their total economic growth since 1984 from the expansion of their trade surpluses—at the expense of the United States. As the United States reduces its deficit, the surpluses of these other countries will come down—and they will be thrown into recession unless they stimulate domestic demand. They should do it for purely domestic reasons, but if they do not do it, the world economy will slow down to less than the 3 percent growth threshold needed to keep less-developed country exports rising.

Therefore, it is absolutely crucial that the industrial countries work together to continue the correction that was begun in September 1985. Balanced, sustained world economic growth can be assured if Germany, Japan, and the others in the industrial world pick up their share of economic expansion and move forward during these next few years.

In the longer run, more effective world economic management is going to require a new international monetary system. It may be a system of target zones, or it may be enhanced multilateral surveillance in the IMF. But whatever it is, we must not limit our thinking about long-run development solutions to narrow-minded questions about what the developing debtor countries must do themselves. We also must look to what the industrial countries must do to provide an environment within which less-developed countries can succeed.

Private Lender Support

There will remain a great need for substantial flows of new capital into the developing countries. But it does not help for the United States to absorb $100 to $150 billion a year from the rest of the world. Brazil was the world's largest debtor country until 1986 when it was replaced by the United States, whose debt is increasing at a faster pace. Latin American capital flight is modest compared to the vast sums attracted by the U.S. market. U.S. fiscal adjustment, then, is an essential element of the world economic picture and that of the Third World. But additional ways must be found to continue at least a modicum of capital flow into the developing debtor countries in order to support export-led opportunities there.

The Baker Plan is a step in a good direction, but it is grossly inadequate. Probably two to three times the amount of money envisaged in the Baker Plan is needed to meet even a minimum requirement for capital flow to the debtor countries; there must be enough economic growth to permit the countries to maintain internal stability, develop a political consensus, and sustain the responsible adjustment paths that most of them have launched already. In my opinion, $15 to $20 billion a year is needed; the Baker Plan envisages $10 billion a year.

What is needed is a significant amount beyond what is envisaged currently. It is neither likely nor desirable that additional funding will come from the commercial banks. They are understandably worried; their lending is short term and at floating interest rates with a great deal of volatility. Other sources of capital should be tapped.

Before the first oil shock in 1973, about three-quarters of all the external capital going into the developing world was public capital. Only one-fourth was private. After the oil shock, the ratio reversed: three-fourths private, mainly commercial banks, and only one-fourth official. A better balance is needed. A half-and-half balance would lead to a more stable structure and level of flow into the Third World. National budgets cannot be tapped anymore, although national export credit agencies now should be providing a great deal more credit to the debtor countries. Rather, the international financial institutions, particularly the World Bank, should become much more aggressive.

The Multilateral Banks

The World Bank should aim immediately to raise its annual lending levels by $4 to $5 billion and should accelerate its disbursements. A new general capital increase should be agreed upon to increase the resources of the World Bank by 50 to 100 percent—and the sooner, the better.

Of course, getting congressional approval for the annual U.S. contributions to the World Bank and other agencies is a difficult task requiring a great deal of prudence and skill in domestic politics. But it must be remembered that U.S. contributions to the World Bank can be done with minimal or zero cost to the budget. Furthermore, every dollar the United States has paid into the World Bank permits $60 of loans. When co-financing by private lenders is added, that figure exceeds $100. In short, the leverage is enormous, and the budget cost is small. Even in an era of Gramm-Rudman and budget austerity, one would hope that Congress would see the wisdom of taking this path.

There are other options for the World Bank. The World Bank holds $20 billion in cash reserves. This is too high when many of the bank's clients are in dire straits and some are actually out of funds. The bank easily could develop safe procedures for transferring a substantial share of its liquid holdings to debtor countries that were implementing responsible policy adjustments. Such an action, obviously, could help alleviate many countries' short-term debt problems.

The International Monetary Fund has been derelict as well. It has the tools to address the reserve and liquidity shortage worldwide due to the Third World debt problem. The IMF should allocate special drawing rights (SDRs) on a substantial level—$10 to $15 billion a year for a few years—to replenish the shortage of reserves.

A major effort also is needed to find ways to tap new sources of private, long-term capital. There are literally tens of trillions of dollars now held around the world by pension funds, insurance companies, mutual funds, and the like; these funds are being invested in a wide range of markets around the world. Even if only a fraction of 1 percent of that money were channeled into the debtor developing countries, this would help them with their capital shortage.

Redirecting capital in this way doubtless will require policy changes on the part of the debtor countries to make them more attractive to potential lenders. A recent Institute for International Economics publication entitled *Financial Intermediation Beyond the Debt Crisis* developed almost a dozen new techniques that could be used. Commodity-linked bonds, indexed bonds, liberalized equity markets within debtor countries, opened up purchases of real estate by foreigners—all of these are techniques the World Bank and the IMF could promote. Such vehicles could provide $1 to $2 billion a year each—sums that would mount up and significantly enhance the external capital availability for these countries. These steps can broaden the portfolio and diversify the amount and nature of funds coming into the debtor countries.

The "Ringmaster"

How does one put all this together? As we have seen, changes are needed by the debtor countries, by the industrial countries, and by the private lenders. The problem is with the implementation of the Baker Plan, which can be likened to a three-ring circus without a ringmaster. Each of the three groups is being asked to do something significant, but nobody is organizing or orchestrating the three efforts. Each group is maximizing its negotiating position and waiting to see what the other two groups do. Despite some progress, there have been few results.

In the first stage of the debt crisis in 1982 and 1983, the IMF was the ringmaster with a strong supporting role from the U.S. government. The IMF pulled the various actors and elements together. This was appropriate because the response to the crisis was economic stabilization, and the IMF was the appropriate agency to address that.

But the IMF is not the correct agency to lead the effort now. We must look for longer-term development, growth strategies, and longer-term capital flows. The World Bank is the natural ringmaster now, and it should take the lead, bring the actors together, and try to fashion a long-term development solution to the crisis.

chapter twelve

The View from the Banks

William R. Rhodes

In the summer of 1980, I chaired a bank advisory committee that was negotiating the restructuring of Nicaragua's foreign commercial-bank debt. At the time, sovereign debt restructuring was a fairly isolated phenomenon. Since the Nicaraguan agreement was signed, much of Latin America has been involved in dramatic debt restructuring efforts, and a new, third phase of the crisis has begun.

The Three Phases of the Crisis

The first phase of the debt crisis began in August 1982, when the challenge was to help debtor nations meet their short-term liquidity needs with new money while these nations restructured and adjusted their economies. For those countries that made progress in their initial adjustment, there has been a second phase, consisting of multiyear restructuring agreements that postpone principal repayment until it represents a smaller proportion of larger, growing national economies. Multiyear restructuring agreements have been negotiated with Ecuador, Mexico, Yugoslavia, the Dominican Republic, Venezuela, and Uruguay.

Consequently, a number of the countries affected by debt repayment problems are recovering economically. As a whole, those countries involved in restructuring have been growing at about 3 percent a year. Current account deficits have declined to 2 percent of gross domestic product, which is better than that of many nations whose creditworthiness has remained unquestioned. Such progress has prepared the way for the third phase, the gradual return to the voluntary markets, a stage that some have called "voluntary lending with a push," as countries adopt policies that foster stable growth without excessive inflation.

Growth became the focus of public discussion in October 1985 when U.S. Treasury Secretary James Baker outlined his initiative to increase lending by multilateral development banks and commercial banks to countries that adopted policies to promote growth-related structural adjustment. Since then, hundreds of representatives from commercial banks, multilateral development banks, debtor nations, and creditor nations have been trying to translate the broad plan into specific country agreements. In March 1986, the World Bank announced plans to lend a total of $1.5 billion to Latin American countries, thus reflecting its commitment to the kind of growth-based lending that is the goal of the Baker Initiative.

As we move ahead, capital inflows to Latin America should be more balanced than they were before the onset of the debt crisis, when cross-border lending by commercial banks for balance-of-payments purposes became such an historically large share. Countries will go to the markets for project finance: co-financing by the commercial banks with the World Bank, the Inter-American Development Bank, and other regional development banks; bond issues, more and more in currencies other than the dollar; and more trade finance. Many of the loans will be for specific projects with the promise of identifiable return. Some existing debt will be exchanged for equity.

Agreements with Uruguay and Colombia, negotiated before the Baker Initiative, are prototypes for the kind of lending we will see in phase three. Uruguay has received commitments on the first voluntary loan by commercial banks to any Latin American country since the debt crisis began. A group of banks has agreed to make a $45 million loan for a hydroelectric project; that sum will be matched by $45 million from the World Bank.

This co-financing agreement is substantially over-subscribed. Among its approximately thirty participants are a number of banks that have never made loans to Uruguay. Clearly, many banks are willing to lend to Latin American borrowers when conditions are right.

The special case of Colombia provides us with another preview of the Baker Initiative, or phase-three loan. Unlike many other less-developed countries involved in the debt crisis, Colombia never missed an interest or principal payment. Nevertheless, it has encountered the same marketplace reluctance as those nations that have missed payments. On December 17, 1985, Colombia signed a $1 billion syndication, mainly for export-related coal and oil projects, with a monitoring agreement with the IMF. Such loans are designed to support the structural adjustment of a country's economy.

Building on this foundation, and as part of the Baker Initiative, the bank advisory committees increasingly will help countries develop proposals for commercial bank financing as part of integrated packages involving the various participants. These proposals might include such approaches as financing with options for onlending, relending, and equity investment, as well as co-financing and parallel lending with the multilateral development banks. Additionally, commercial banks are exploring new ideas for debt instruments and for mutual funds that could provide vehicles for the return of flight capital.

A Closer Look at Phase Three

Of the countries whose bank advisory committees I chair or co-chair, Brazil, for one, has had two excellent years on the external side. A $12.5 billion trade surplus in 1985 followed a record $13.1 billion surplus in 1984. At the end of 1985, the current account deficit was close to equilibrium, and cash reserves stood at almost $9 billion.

In March 1986, the Brazilian government and the advisory committee completed negotiations on an agreement covering $31 billion of debt to commercial banks, thereby sharply reducing spreads on $15.5 billion. Briefly, the agreement involves restructuring approximately $6 billion of 1985 maturities and rolling over $9.5 billion of 1986 maturities, with an interest rate 1⅛ percentage points greater than the cost of funds. This is a drop from an average of more than 2 percent that Brazil had been paying on this debt. In addition, the agreement eliminates the banks' option of linking the interest rate spread to the U.S. prime rate (which tends to be higher than domestic market rates), thereby reducing further the cost of this debt to Brazil. The debt for 1985 will be repaid during seven years, with payments beginning in 1991. Trade and interbank lines totaling approximately $15.5 billion will be extended for about a year. We hope this short-term agreement will lead to a multiyear restructuring.

Unfortunately, the external progress that made this agreement possible has not yet been matched in Brazil's internal economy. To be sure, growth in 1985, at approximately 8 percent, was among the world's highest. Yet, 1985 saw inflation of 230 percent, and in the first two months of 1986 that rate more than doubled.

With this new burst of inflation as a backdrop, President Sarney announced the dramatic Cruzado Plan to meet head on Brazil's decades-old problem of high inflation. If successful, the plan could set the stage for years of sustained growth in the region's largest economy. This new program bodes well for the Brazilian government's desire for an early return to the voluntary markets.

Mexico, after an initially successful adjustment program begun in late 1982, had a disappointing economic performance in 1985, which was exacerbated by the devastation of the earthquakes. The sharp drop in oil prices, if sustained in time, will reduce foreign currency earnings significantly. Also of concern is the need for the country to improve the internal investment environment in order to reverse capital flows.

Begun in 1985, Argentina's Austral Program has helped bring inflation under control. The consumer price index, which rose 31 percent during the month of June 1985, rose by 79 percent for all of 1986. In support of Argentina's structural-adjustment efforts, the World Bank announced a $350 million sectoral loan for agriculture. Argentina made the third drawdown under its $4.2 billion commercial bank new money facility, for $600 million, by April 1986, following its IMF drawdown of 236 million SDRs on March 14.

Peru's arrearages to commercial banks on public sector debt stretch back to before 1985 and have reached about $450 million, although the country's reserves stand at about $1.5 billion. On March 12, 1986, the Peruvian government told its advisory committee that it would make a partial interest payment; in addition, the government indicated that a restructuring proposal was in the works.

At the end of February 1986, the government of Uruguay reached agreement with its bank advisory committee on a multiyear restructuring as well as the $45 million voluntary co-financing loan with the World Bank. The multiyear agreement covers maturities from the beginning of 1985 through the end of 1989. This accounts for nearly $2 billion of the $2.2 billion that the government owes to commercial banks.

The Private Sector and Industrialized Nations

In addition to these changes, a number of countries already have taken significant steps toward structural adjustment to encourage capital formation and capital inflows, with emphasis on the private sector. Brazil has sold some $400 million in stock of Petrobras, the state oil company, and shares in sixteen other state-owned companies. Mexico has sold a state-owned hotel chain and recently announced plans to market as many as two hundred other state companies. Most significantly, Mexico has joined the General Agreement on Tariffs and Trade (GATT). Ecuador, too, has sold a number of state-owned companies.

One hopes that the countries of Latin America see such measures as only the first steps in structural adjustment. Bolder measures are needed, with realistic exchange and interest rates a key, to reduce pressure for capital flight and to help make domestic savings a far greater factor in financing development. Such measures also will encourage foreign direct investment, thus stimulating growth and decreasing reliance on foreign borrowings. The World Bank and the IMF are exploring the possibilities for foreign direct investment in consultation with private international corporations.

Implicit in the Baker Initiative is a commitment by the industrialized nations to the same kind of economic policies as the debtor countries. The goals of these policies include lower inflation, which should lead to lower interest rates, and sustained growth, which along with continued access to world export markets would enable debtor countries to further build their foreign exchange resources. Industrialized nations should maintain their export cover for countries with IMF and bank agreements and be prepared to negotiate multiyear restructurings along the lines of commercial bank packages.

The overall economic picture has many uncertainties. Oil prices, commodity prices, exchange rates, and the threat of protectionism all remain important question marks, along with the direction of interest rates. The interest rate picture improved in early 1986. The London Interbank Offered Rate (LIBOR) fell some 450 basis points from mid-1984. Each hundred basis point drop in interest rates saves Mexico between $700 and $800 million in payments to commercial banks, with a slightly higher figure for Brazil and some $300 million for Argentina. Growth in the industrialized nations is crucial, as it fuels demand for less-developed country exports.

Another crucial question is whether the Latin American countries have the political will to continue the steps necessary to return their economies to health. In Latin America, many countries are undertaking economic adjustment during one of the region's most significant political transformations in generations, with widespread movement from military government to democracy. Argentina, Uruguay, and Brazil are examples of newly democratic governments taking strong measures to resolve their economic problems.

Helping Latin America realize its considerable potential will take more of the hard work, commitment, and mutual understanding by all parties that we have seen since 1982. Although there are bound to be setbacks ahead, as there have been in the past, I believe that a number of countries have made, and will continue to make, real progress toward regaining their creditworthiness and achieving sustainable economic growth in the years ahead.

chapter thirteen

Four Feasible Ways to Ameliorate the Debt Burden

Albert Fishlow

A correct analysis of the debt problem needs to begin by recognizing three points about the origin and evolution of the debt crisis. First, the effort to ameliorate the debt crisis does not constitute a reward for profligacy or errors in internal policies. The problem did not arise simply because thirty countries around the world simultaneously made the same mistakes in their domestic policies. There was a common, external set of factors that helped provoke the crisis.

Second, discussions about capital flight should recognize that responsible estimates such as those of the Bank of England suggest that capital flight is perhaps $80 billion out of an investment in Latin America of $400 billion. In other words, fully 80 percent of the loans remain invested in the region and in many cases have been utilized productively. Furthermore, in virtually all Latin American countries, investment rates increased during the 1970s, and this made possible a considerable part of the adjustment in the 1980s. Brazil's success in increasing exports in 1984 and reducing imports since 1980 would not have been possible without the accumulation of debt during the 1970s.

Third, the evolution of the debt crisis should not leave one complacent about the future of the developing world or the global economy. The major task during the first phase of the debt crisis was to reestablish the integrity of the international financial system. Although this task was essential, there was a serious cost incurred as the international community shored up the system.

That cost was substantially lower growth in Latin America and more broadly in the developing world. Since the onset of the crisis, growth has been substantially less than historical levels. Latin America is not a region of "basket cases." Throughout the postwar period, Latin American countries experienced positive per capita income growth that indeed was accelerating in the 1960s and 1970s.

The present phase of the debt crisis has been concerned with restoring a basis for sustained and interdependent development of the debtor countries. Although there are reasons to be optimistic, there is no excuse for complacency. More rapid economic growth in the industrialized countries, lower interest rates, and more rapid growth in trade provide grounds for hope, but these are not substitutes for other important efforts or excuses for assuming that the problem will go away.

The Baker Plan: A Critique

Let me identify three important problems with the Baker Plan. First, implicit in the Baker Plan is a continuation of the past sequencing of adjustment. The burden falls on the debtor countries to demonstrate that wide-ranging structural reforms are in place. Only then would financing begin. However, adequate financing is necessary to permit those reforms and to underwrite the higher rates of investment necessary for continuing export and income growth.

Second, the magnitude of the assistance contemplated by the Baker Plan simply would not permit the growth that it promised. If the goal is to stimulate capital inflows at the rate of 2 to 3 percent of the region's gross product, then $20 billion a year will be needed, not $10 billion. That makes an extraordinary difference. Ten billion dollars a year permits the adjustment of balance of payments, not growth. An additional $10 billion is necessary for growth. The additional $10 billion permits import liberalization, for example, which is needed desperately in Latin America. Can those countries afford to liberalize imports now when they must precariously defend their balance of payments and use their foreign exchange to pay interest? The answer is obviously no. But how will these countries be able to grow in an efficient, sustained way without liberalization? The orders of magnitude of finance have to be at the center of the discussion. There is a substantial difference between growth of 3.5 to 4 percent that fails to absorb the new entrants into the labor force and the 5 to 5.5 percent that is necessary and corresponds to the past trend of development in the region.

Third, the way that the issues of conditionality and long-term reform have been posed do a fundamental injustice to Latin America and other developing countries. To suggest that Latin American countries will follow the right policies only under external tutelage and a short leash reflects the paternalism of the past. There has been an unstated but mistaken assumption that finance ministers want to do the right thing, but presidents want to do the wrong thing. Therefore, someone must tell the finance ministers what they have to make the presidents do.

That may have been an appropriate view when populist tendencies were prominent in the region, but it is inappropriate now for two reasons. Today many Latin American presidents are democratic, more informed about economic policy, and committed to responsible reform. In turn, finance ministers in democratic and civilian participatory regimes are aware of the need for sustainable growth that will permit them to stay in power for years rather than months. Electorates will have to be informed and learn to look ahead. They must become capable of resisting excessive and inconsistent populist demands, so that responsible policies are rewarded correctly. External pressure is a very imperfect substitute that cannot be relied upon for the long haul. It is as likely to provoke popular resistance as to assure compliance with adjustment. Recent reforms in Brazil and Argentina have gone well beyond what the IMF would have proposed. These two countries were able to undertake reforms because their government enjoyed broad domestic political support and could explain the new policies.

New conceptions of conditionality are necessary that are more consistent with a growth than an austerity objective and that give greater scope to self-monitoring and continual policy correction.

Long-Term Development Strategies

Implicit in any discussion of long-term reform is a preferred development strategy. One should be cautious about generalizations. The one country in Latin America that comes closest to having fulfilled the conditions of the free market development strategy is Chile. Chile had an open market for capital and trade with low tariffs, a trivial government deficit, and directed credit to the private sector. Today, Chile has one of the highest ratios of debt to gross domestic product in the region to show for its pains, not to mention sharp declines in income per capita.

There are no simple, magic formulas. Still, three elements seem central to an effective development strategy for most Latin American debtors in the latter 1980s and the 1990s. First, there needs to be a better balance between the public and private sector. The central problem is not that the public sector is too large; rather, it is the fact that the public and private sectors do not cooperate. The public sector is large in Taiwan and Korea, but it complements and facilitates the private sector. The issue is not the size of the public sector per se but whether its activities crowd out the finance and initiative of the private sector.

Second, Latin America needs more symmetrical integration in both the capital and trade markets of the world. For a long period of time, Latin America has had free capital markets and too much protection against imports. It has biased itself in the direction of too much finance and too few exports. In other regions, integration into the international economy has proceeded in a more symmetrical fashion.

Balance is preferable to a simple export-led strategy driven by continuing penetration of other countries' markets. Brazil often is cited as a successful example of such an orientation. Brazil's growth, in 1985 at 8 percent, has come from the domestic market. Export receipts in 1985 were smaller than in 1984. Rising real wages and increased internal demand were more important in explaining Brazil's economic growth than its stagnant exports.

More generally, the economic orientation of debtor countries should no longer follow polar formulas like export promotion or import substitution. A conjunction of both is needed. In the last analysis, Latin America must earn more of its foreign exchange through trade than through finance. This requirement is clear to everyone in the region and to most outside observers. Virtually every country in the region is committed to such a change. For the larger countries, the internal market will remain an important asset to be exploited as an efficient industrial sector is developed, and this internal development will permit subsequent exports of those manufactured products. Latin America will never be like Korea, which exports 50 percent of its industrial sector product. On the other hand, Latin America certainly should be a region in which export growth keeps pace with product growth.

A third important, and often overlooked, factor is the problem of inequality of the income distribution within the region. The new democracies and rising expectations confront internal concentrations of income that are among the highest in the developing world. In the early 1980s, there has been an exacerbation of inequality by virtue of the decline in real wages and the rise in real interest rates. One of the very important economic management problems in Latin America in the near future will be responsible settlement of demands on the part of those who have been deprived during these difficult years. Consumption growth will have to be weighed against an expansion of internal savings and needed investment. Real wages must allow for rates of profit that stimulate production and maintenance of sustainable growth through continuing investment.

An Alternative to the Baker Plan: Four Proposals

It is only through economic growth that one is able to reconcile the need for a rising standard of living and continuing service of a large overhanging debt. That is why adequate growth—rather than mere adjustment in the balance of payments—is so essential to any resolution of the debt problem. Although the Baker Plan starts from that premise, its three basic features offer a somewhat eccentric design that will win few awards either for functionality or for beauty. The Baker Plan is a stool with three legs of very different lengths.

One "leg" is provisional—it is the promise of better OECD growth policies, in spite of the reality that coordination remains limited and the U.S. fiscal deficit remains much too large. The second leg is unsteady—it is the *hope* for more money, rather than a demonstrated conviction that the required $20 billion a year will be available. The third leg is too long and is something of a big stick—it is the insistence upon immediate action by the developing countries to demonstrate commitment to adjustment of their balance of payments and to structural reform. In the end, these countries will have to do all of the adjustment if hopes and promises do not materialize.

A better job of construction within the confines of a nondebt forgiveness approach is possible. What is now required—as a result of the large efforts already made by debtor countries—is a demonstrable commitment to greater participation by the creditor governments. In the Baker Plan, significant contributions by the industrial country governments are the missing leg. Yet they must be an integral part of the equation if Latin America is going to see the kind of development it wants and needs and that adequate finance can make possible.

What should the governments do? First, they should modify the International Monetary Fund's compensatory financing facilities to extend to interest rates. Can we not guarantee to the developing countries that if interest rates, which are currently at reduced but still high levels relative to export price movements, increase, there will automatically be relief available? That will establish a ceiling to debt service efforts. Such commitment would be a perfect example of seizing upon the better present conditions to assure a more certain future. This can limit the vulnerability in the large debt exposure that the Baker Plan implicitly accepts.

Second, creditor governments must make a continuing commitment to much larger official lending. In the 1970s, there was a sudden flow of private capital that overwhelmed official lending; this was an aberration. But commercial banks are not development institutions; they *became* development institutions because there was no creditor government participation. Omitting a role for creditor governments at this time repeats that same mistake while at the same time imposing continuing large debt service payments to the private creditors.

Third, a new "reverse oil facility" should be established to provide additional financing. When Saudi Arabia and the other oil-producing countries received a large trade surplus, most agreed that recycling petrodollars would benefit the countries must adversely affected and the world economy.

Presently, Japan and Germany are benefiting from the shifting currents of world trade, and this too presents both a problem and an opportunity. The time has come to consider a new reverse oil facility redistributing contributions from Japan and Germany to some of the developing country oil-exporters that have been adversely affected. Improvement in oil prices could allow the facility—still financed from the surplus countries—to extend its operations more broadly. This is a temporary matter and, of course, should not substitute for measures to reduce the present large trade surpluses.

Fourth, the banks should consider multiyear commitments of new resources subject to subsequent revision if adjustment proves unsatisfactory. This changes the burden of proof. The right framework for policies that produce growth cannot be created if banks and debtor countries spend the entire year negotiating loans only to reach agreements in December for an amount of money that was needed the previous January. What countries need is an element of certainty. The debtor countries need to know what funds are going to be available because meaningful reforms require longer-term investment projects.

These proposals add up to reducing the now large, and continuing, resource transfers of the region on the order of $20 to $30 billion a year through larger return flows of new money. More debt will be feasible as a solution only if nominal interest rates continue their descent and are not offset by deteriorating export prices. Then the inertial growth of debt due to accumulating interest payments will not outstrip the growth of developing country products and exports, and debt ratios will decline. Countries can also have greater assurance that the domestic application of foreign loans will yield returns that will more than repay the costs of borrowing. In addition, stable and continuous growth in the OECD countries will be necessary, if the vulnerability created by a large debt overhang is not to stifle developing country progress.

Otherwise, new debt is not a solution; it adds to the problem. Inevitably, one will have to shift to debt reduction plans that necessarily will impose greater cost on creditors. The Baker approach, as here amplified to incorporate adequate lending, is more generous to the commercial banks. But they may well have to bear a larger share of the burden of the losses arising from the present debt unless the external environment improves.

The Judgment of History

What will historians say when they look back on this period? History will not concern itself with the intricacies of bank regulation or the rationalizations of why governments found it impossible to do more. History will not focus upon the technicalities associated with one particular debt arrangement or another. History will focus on the absence of a response to the debt crisis of 1982 and the continuing problem.

In the early 1920s, President Coolidge confronted both the inter-Allied war debts and the German reparations problems. The British suggested offsetting cancellation of both debts because of the magnitude of the loans and the implications of the financial transfers necessary for the European economy. Coolidge responded, "They hired the money, didn't they?" That was the end of the conversation. In his mind, a sacred contractual obligation had been incurred and could not be altered.

A different response was provided by the Alliance for Progress. It was launched in 1961 when Latin American growth had slowed and limited availability of private finance prejudiced possibilities of development. Suddenly, as a result of political preoccupation with Cuba, official resources were provided on an unprecedented basis. All the excuses of a few years earlier—excuses decrying the impossibility of such an effort—evaporated. They became irrelevant in the face of a conscious commitment to a new cooperative undertaking of potential historic importance.

The tasks of mobilizing support and taking a decision in favor of action are now more difficult. One cannot appeal to the threat of Fidel Castro and widespread guerrilla subversion in the region. Because there is no external threat and no overt anti-Americanism, the United States seems unable to galvanize itself to respond to the debt problem. Yet what is at stake is no less central to the evolution of the hemisphere and the political relationship between the United States and Latin America. Democracy, defense of human rights, and peaceful settlement of disputes are all at risk if countries do not experience the growth and development necessary to absorb growing labor forces. History will judge us harshly for our insensitivity to the debt problem and our lack of political will to take the steps necessary to assure its resolution. Thus far we have succeeded only in coping and inverting the crisis to a chronic problem.

Comments and Discussion on Part Two

The second discussion panel, co-chaired by former President Jimmy Carter and former Senator Howard Baker (now White House chief of staff), included symposium participants J. Gustave Speth, Pedro-Pablo Kuczynski, David C. Mulford, C. Fred Bergsten, William Rhodes, and Albert Fishlow. Questions also were accepted from the audience.

Jimmy Carter: What will happen in Latin America if the region does not receive an adequate amount of capital, at least to service its debts?

Pedro-Pablo Kuczynski: The debt problem has persisted, but it has also changed in some ways. For example, Brazil clearly is getting off the debt train not just because of domestic growth, but also because of export growth.

The most immediate problems are clearly with the oil countries. It is not just the drop in export revenues, but the uncertainty of future oil prices. For example, if a price of $14 were to prevail for the rest of the year, then the problem is much less significant than if oil stayed at $10. Mexico has reserves to ride out a short-term problem, but it does not have enough reserves to ride out a long-term problem. Everyone expects a package of economic and fiscal measures from Mexico, and that will influence what happens to nontraditional exports and border trade and tourism.

Venezuela, on the other hand, has a very high level of reserves, and it can offset problems for a year or so. The oil price is only a small part of Peru's problem, which extends back ten to twenty years. Domestic solutions are more important than external ones. Foreign exchange reserves are, in fact, quite high.

In short, all three of these cases are different. I agree that more concerted action is needed; but I doubt that the World Bank is as efficient an organization to mount a long-term program as the International Monetary Fund was for launching its short-term program. The IMF is a much smaller organization with a very strong staff; the World Bank is a large, diffuse organization with many missions. Although I am not saying that it cannot be done, I think the bank will have difficulty adjusting to this new role.

113

Preventing a Repetition

Howard Baker: It seems to me that we still are not fully addressing the question of how we got where we are, how to get out, and how to avoid such problems in the future. Extensive borrowing by countries of this hemisphere occurred because there was a lot of money to be lent; there was a great unmet demand in Latin America, and commercial banks in particular seemed to think the region was a good market. The borrowers thought it was a good opportunity.

But it also seems to me that, consciously or unconsciously, we assumed that oil prices were not going to go down significantly and that no one was going to mount a major war against inflation. But both those things did happen.

I noted Mr. Mulford's remark that the principle rationale for the Baker Plan, which I think is an excellent initiative, is that countries will be able to borrow enough additional money to carry through the reforms that are necessary. What are the odds that we can avoid the same mistakes we made before? How can we assure stability if we go forward with additional financing and additional loans? How can we encourage reforms without being resented by the very countries that we are attempting to help?

David C. Mulford: The best guard for the future against a recurrence of this situation is our own experience. The debtor countries recognize that they overborrowed. The commercial banks realize that they overlent. Both parties recognize that there are extreme risks in this time of excessive activity, and I think it will be a long time before we see this repeated.

Is there enough money available? Questions of this sort are really at the heart of the matter.

Reform will come because it is wanted by the debtors themselves as the basis for sustained growth. They also recognize that the answer is not just more debt. Earlier I made the point that some additional finance—I did not say debt—is going to be necessary. Some of it inevitably will be debt, especially in the near term, until the adjustment is accomplished.

From the viewpoint of a practitioner with years of experience in financial markets, let me simply run down a list for you outlining where money comes from. First, are we going to look to the industrial governments for additional funds? The United States, however, is facing Gramm-Rudman. It is engaged in a deficit reduction exercise that the entire world, including the debtor nations, has wanted it to undertake for some time and that the United States has recognized it must do. On what basis can we justify increasing outlays for Latin American debt against this backdrop? Where is it to end? What about U.S. farmers, what about the U.S. energy industry, what about all the people in the United States who also are caught in the same adjustment to a deinflationary situation, to changing economic circumstances? Does that mean we extend the same sort of approach to them? If so, we can forget about deficit reduction.

Among the boards of commercial banks, there are a lot of directors who do not want to put up new money to countries that have not yet made reforms. There is a practical limitation there we have to face. The countries themselves already have said they do not want to just go on accumulating additional debt. I might point out that we got into this business in the first place, in part, by an excessive amount of finance. We seem to be ignoring that when we propose additional amounts.

Third, regarding the World Bank and other international institutions, we think the resources are adequate. If the World Bank were simply to begin pumping money into Latin America, in order to get money out, the bank would destroy its own creditworthiness as an institution in a very short time. None of us wants to see that. We want to see the World Bank enhance its activities while maintaining the same high standards of creditworthiness and loan quality. The bank's standards are worth preserving.

Next is private investment, something that is too often ignored. If Latin America adopted a different, more open policy toward direct investment, there would be additional flows, and this is not debt, but equity. If employed effectively by private sector investors, they will create jobs that facilitate the adjustment.

Finally, there is the reflow by the citizens of the countries. Again, this is not debt. If such reflows were encouraged by the appropriate investment climate, interest rate structure, exchange rate, and general reform in the economies, people would "vote" by bringing their money back.

But when it comes to the issue of reform, how do you actually accomplish it? In my experience, reform can be very difficult. The United States, as Senator Baker has said, cannot and should not be in the position of dictating economic packages for the debtor nations. They are turning to the IMF and to the World Bank, but they are drawing primarily on their own resources, designing their own plans and programs. We hope we can be helpful in that process, but the reform lies with the debtor countries. It is in their interest and within their power to make the reforms that will bring growth and recapture financial resources already owned by their own citizens, instead of acquiring additional debt. If this works, the debt burden will again become manageable within growing economies.

U.S. Priorities

Jimmy Carter: The thing that continues to prey on my mind is the assessment of priorities. Our nation is obsessed with how to deal with Khadafy, or whether to spend $100 million for Contra aid in Nicaragua. Senator Bradley put these concerns in good perspective when he pointed out that the interest payments by the Latin American countries to creditor nations total about $100 million *every day*—but we are obsessed with the peripheral issues as a political priority, almost to the exclusion of forming a genuine partnership between the creditor and debtor nations. Most of the goals I have heard expressed, either by representatives of the debtor nations or others, have centered on the question of whether the countries will be able to pay the interest on the debt—or the service charges for rolling over the debt—in future years.

This leaves almost unaddressed the basic fact that among some of the poorer nations on earth, those struggling for a better life for their people, we have an unprecedented drain of capital flowing to the richest nations on earth. In the last four years, we have had an average of about $40 billion a year flowing from the debtor nations in Latin America to the creditor nations. With the reduced interest rates that might come from lower oil prices, this sum might be reduced to $30 billion a year. But it is going to be a continuing burden just to pay interest—even without addressing any payments on the principal.

These interest payments from 1982 through 1985 together with estimated capital flight add up to a figure about fifteen times greater than the total spent on the Marshall Plan. This money is coming *from* the countries in need *to* the richer nations on earth. It apparently is a permanent economic load on countries struggling for a better life. In the long run, how is this problem going to be addressed even under optimum circumstances?

Lessons from the Past

C. Fred Bergsten: In a sense, it is easier to handle this problem in the long run than in the short run. If you look at the history of economic development, going back into the nineteenth century, most developing countries borrowed heavily. They piled up external debt and interest obligations that seemed high at the time. The United States, for example, was a debtor country throughout the nineteenth century. The United states accumulated heavy external debt, but it maintained the kind of economic dynamism and export-oriented growth that enabled it to do so.

Of course, some countries did not. A number of countries defaulted, not just once but numerous times in the nineteenth century. In the 1930s, it happened again. The issue therefore is what enabled some to make it and some not to make it. It had a lot to do with resource endowment and natural capabilities, but it also was determined by the countries' own policies and the world environment.

In the 1930s and in different periods of financial panic in the nineteenth century, there were many defaults. This is why I put so much emphasis on the responsibility of the industrial countries, not just the United States, but Japan, Germany, and others, to manage the world economy in a stable, growing, and effective way. If that is done—and I realize this is a big "if"—then I have a reasonable degree of confidence that the interest burden will not be overwhelming.

As we pointed out, Brazil is paying $9 to $10 billion of interest a year right now and really doing swimmingly. Brazilians are doing well partly because of their own policies—they keep their exchange rates competitive—but also because they have been able to expand their exports and their trade surplus by $8 billion from 1983 through 1985. Therefore, they obviated the foreign exchange constraint and have been able to boost domestic demand and get the economy moving. It is a combination of two things: the internal policies and the external environment.

Some countries do face a constraint because of their interest payments. But even in those cases, we should question the result—the "general equilibrium result," as economists would put it—if there were either repudiation or a unilateral forgiveness. Probably, the "forgiven" countries' access to new capital would be cut off or at least sharply diminished for a long time afterward. So the apparent attractiveness of reducing cash flow by somehow limiting or even eliminating interest payments looks very different in light of the impact on one's overall position. Even with the Alan García option of limiting interest payments to some share of export earnings, you have to ask what that does to capital inflow. In the Peruvian case, the evidence is growing that capital inflow is drying up and that the net effect is nothing like the gross gain that was expected.

Now, these are the consequences even without extremes: a country written out of the world economy, having its foreign assets seized. Except in cases of world depression—as in the 1930s—the better course is to try expanding exports. As long as exports are growing faster than the real rate of interest, the debt burden is being reduced, making the maximum possible contribution to development efforts

Albert Fishlow: It is very important to recognize the uniqueness of the current crisis. We are trying to deal with an excess of debt without the usual historical context of repudiation, inflation, or some kind of revolution. If we look back, the accumulated debt at the end of the nineteenth century was made tolerable by the inflation of World War I. It was the Mexican revolution that led to repudiation of the accumulated debt there during the late nineteenth century and beginning of the twentieth. What we are trying to do now is much harder, and we are trying to do it on a concerted basis, which is why the responsibility of the industrialized countries must be recognized.

Countries can grow out of their debt burden, but the key issue is what is expected at the beginning. The reverse transfer flow has been responsible for the reduced investment in a variety of countries in the region during the last several years. What the Baker Initiative correctly envisages is the need to turn that trend around. What is unusual about the present circumstance is that it is not the result of a natural process, but of an extraordinarily unnatural process in which there was a growth of private debt on an unprecedented basis—an aberration—and then there was a sudden relapse, in which there was no more capital available.

Case by Case

William Rhodes: We should approach these questions on a case-by-case basis. Most of the foreign funds that went into Brazil were used to diversify: to build an industrial plant, to finance hydroelectric projects, to finance a mineral project in the north. These projects have given Brazilians the export capacity that is leading them back to growth. Their external interest payments came to some $10 billion in 1985. That will be reduced to around $8.8 billion, and Brazilians will probably have a balance-of-trade surplus somewhere in the area of $13 billion. Their reserves are going up. Obviously, Brazil has benefited by recent events.

In the case of Argentina, we have seen a very courageous stance by President Alfonsín. There will be significant progress in time. The Argentines are in the process of reforming their agricultural base, and they just received a loan from the World Bank. There is no doubt that Argentina needs structural adjustment; it has been put off for some time.

As for Mexico, I would like to emphasize first that I think Mexico always has dealt with its foreign debt situation in a very responsible manner. Mexicans are taking steps now to keep their exchange rate on a more realistic basis in order to stem capital flight, and in the months of January and February 1986, they actually had a net inflow. I think Mexico's decision to join GATT was a very necessary one. It is tied in with the trade development program Mexico is working out with the World Bank to diversify its economy.

The industrialized nations have got to continue working to get the real rate of interest down. I think that is key, and I think that it will happen. I am concerned, however, that the industrialized nations do not remove their export cover. This is very important for the less-developed countries throughout Latin America. When we do our multiyear restructurings, it is very important that the industrialized countries join us and restructure the debt that they hold over similarly long periods and with the terms that we are talking about.

Conditionality

Question: With all due respect, politicians do not make reforms until they have to. Reforms are politically painful and difficult. Will new loans postpone the need for reform among countries that need it very badly?

David C. Mulford: It is very important that additional finance be linked to reform, whether it is made by the commercial banks or the World Bank, because lenders want to see the promise of improvement before they lend. Reform is a difficult process, as you have intimated. It will not occur if countries receive a large volume of finance up front or on easy terms. The quality of the lending and the investment, not the volume, will produce results if debtor countries design their own plans and introduce reforms.

Argentina has done something very bold, but it did not do it early in President Alfonsín's administration. The Argentines took the initiative only as the clouds were gathering and things became more and more difficult. Once they acted, they found out what many governments have found out: that taking action in a democracy is often much more popular than the political leader thinks, and the action turns out to have more beneficial results sooner, of a politically valuable type, than does defending the present position and refusing to reform.

C. Fred Bergsten: To underline this last point, the immediate reaction in Brazil to the Cruzado Plan has been an enormous outpouring of support for Brazilian President Sarney. On the question of whether new loans preclude or promote policy reform, I agree with David Mulford. But there is an important additional issue to be addressed. Should lenders go in with the minimum amount necessary to keep things afloat, or should they be fairly generous in rewarding the reform and maybe even helping buy a little more reform at the margin?

It is a little too simplistic to say, "Get the reform first, and then put in money." There is an interaction between the two sides of the equation. If a country has good export-led growth strategies in the long term, the private sector probably will provide as much money as a country would want and could borrow prudently. But in this intermediate period, while we are coming out of the crisis, private lenders still are going to be quite reluctant. So the question is, should the World Bank be lending at annual rates of $12 billion or $18 billion? That $6 billion a year difference represents a 50 percent greater lending level.

I opt for the larger amount to help galvanize the reforms, reward them when taken, and also serve as a demonstration to other countries that reforms will be rewarded. The larger amounts also can buy a little more growth, thus improving the climate to sustain the reforms. I therefore would recommend providing more loans as an important component of the whole strategy.

Albert Fishlow: Whether the reforms are called export-adequate or export-promotion, they are leading to an expansion of imports. The secret of Korea and Taiwan has not been merely a high rate of export growth; it has been a high rate of import growth. You cannot have an efficient export sector if you do not have a large rate of growth of imports. But this cannot be attained with the projected levels of finance at the present time.

The Responsibilities of the Surplus Countries

Question: We all have spoken about the need for reform in the debtor countries. Most of us also recognize that there has to be some symmetry on the part of some industrialized countries. Beyond wishful thinking, what are the tools whereby we can get West Germany and Japan to expand their economies?

C. Fred Bergsten: Since 1984, Japan and Germany have achieved at least half of their total economic growth from the improvement of their trade surpluses. Now, it is inevitable that the United States is going to reduce its trade deficit, now running at $150 billion, by something like $100 or $150 billion during the next few years. The Plaza agreement of September 1985 is aimed exactly at that. If the U.S. deficit is going to decline by $100 billion, the deficit is going to decline by $100 billion, the Japanese and German surpluses are going to decline by close to $50 billion each. So instead of getting half their economic growth from that expansion, they are both going to lose the growth, which, in terms of their economies, may be very substantial.

If they do nothing in response, their unemployment rates will rise enormously. Germany's unemployment is already very high—9 or 10 percent. It would rise another 3 or 4 percentage points. Japan's rate would probably double. For purely internal reasons of avoiding severe recession, once these two countries perceive that the United States is serious and is going to adjust, then they will have to take offsetting measures of domestic demand.

They must act for world economic stability as well, but the internal pressures, as always, will take precedence.

The second point is that Japan and Germany do have a choice. Either they can let their currencies keep rising further and further, or they can stimulate their domestic demand. If the Japanese take no internal expansionary measures, I predict that the yen will go to 130 within the next year. Such a rise would eliminate a large part of the Japanese export industry. At some point, then, they must realize that they really face a tradeoff.

In fact, the reason the Germans reduced their discount rate in the spring of 1986 was that they were worried that the deutsche mark would otherwise continue to rise sharply. The Reagan administration was quite blunt in putting pressure on Japan and particularly Germany; the message was that the mark will keep rising, hurting Germany's international competitiveness quite substantially, unless the Germans took alternative measures—like cuts in interest rates—to stimulate their domestic economy. That approach worked; I think it also will work with the Japanese. But fiscal policy in both countries needs to be expanded, and in my view, that should be the next objective of the Group of Five.

Howard Baker: I am pessimistic. For sociological reasons, because of the island mentality of the Japanese, it is highly unlikely that they are going to change their taste in products, goods, and services and begin buying products made in other countries such as the United States or Latin America. It is unlikely that we are going to be able to compete to a large extent in the Japanese home market.

Given that, the question before us becomes very relevant. What will the Japanese do if the currency readjustment and other factors lead to a decline in the value of their exports to the United States and to the countries of this hemisphere and Western Europe? I do not know what they will do, but I do not believe they are going to increase the rate of their purchases and imports significantly.

Pedro-Pablo Kuczynski: I do not know how you convince people to do things they do not want to do, but there are two points to be made. First, the realignment of exchange rates by itself already is putting pressure on Japan and Germany. These are the same people who, two or three years ago, were complaining about the very high dollar. Now they are complaining the opposite—the dollar has gone down too much. At this point, of course, they have to reflate their economies. So the market is in some sense taking care of the problem.

Second, it is very important to get the multilateral trade negotiations underway. The European Economic Community (EEC) and Japan are highly protectionist. The only really big market remaining open to the Latin Americans, besides their own, is the U.S. market. There has to be some heat put on the EEC and the Far Eastern countries to open their markets. They are not carrying their share of the burden.

The Bradley Plan

C. Fred Bergsten: Even though I am a strong supporter of Senator Bradley, I think his plan gave too much weight to machinery and too little to substance. He did not really say where he thought any new money to finance debt relief might come from. What he did talk about was setting up new committees. I frankly think the last thing we need is a lot more machinery and committees. We already have too much international machinery, too many meetings, too many groups. What is needed is to use the groups effectively.

The IMF ran a pretty effective show in 1982 and the year or two after that. Mr. Kuczynski raised the question of whether the World Bank was geared to do it now. I agree that there may have to be some change in the orientation, nature, and leadership of the institution, but these things could be done rather quickly under its new president Barber Conable. The issue is how to get existing institutions to address substantive questions.

Question: What did Senator Bradley mean about no more loans?

C. Fred Bergsten: He seemed to be saying we should find ways to relieve the existing debt instead of lending new money. This view is essentially the opposite of what the rest of us are saying because we have a different view of how the international financial system works and what would be more stable in the long run and beneficial to the borrowing countries. I certainly do not advocate a further accumulation of debt for the developing countries, but most forms of debt relief, which focus on capitalization of interest, do the same thing as borrowing new money. They stretch out the payments, but they do not reduce the debt; indeed, they raise it.

Jimmy Carter: In defense of what Bill Bradley said, one of his concerns was that no one now knows who is going to take the initiative to get us over this present hurdle. Fred Bergsten says the World Bank; others say the IMF; and some say the private sector ought to take the initiative. Others say the developing nations ought to take the initiative to reform their internal policies. Others say perhaps it should be some other entity. What Bradley was saying was let us bring a small group of representatives from all of those entities to work together to solve the problem.

part three

The Dialogue on the Debt

chapter fourteen

The Circle in the Debate: A Rapporteur's Report

Richard E. Feinberg

The years prior to 1982 during which the debt was accumulated now seem a distant memory, a golden era during which private bankers were willing to lend almost without limit to apparently strong, growing Latin American economies. The participants in the symposium discussed the origins of the debt crisis but concentrated on the much more immediate and politically pressing theme of the costs of the debt overhang—the sum of damages sustained since the crisis began in the second half of 1982. The symposium participants also discussed the implications of the debt crisis for political stability and U.S.–Latin American relations.

In reviewing efforts to date to cope with the now chronic financial crisis, speakers differed as to the degree of progress; all recognized, however, that the debt problem is far from resolved, and some noted with concern that several serious setbacks had been registered. Speakers therefore devoted substantial time to analyzing recent initiatives and proposing new ideas for improving the management of the debt problem while simultaneously spurring economic growth in Latin America.

Origins of the Debt Crisis

Analyses of the causes behind Latin America's current economic woes generally emphasize one of two elements: vacillations in the international economy or faults in the policies of debtor nations. Observers typically will admit that both factors play a role but often will focus more attention on one set of causes than the other. Not surprisingly, the institutional location or political position of analysts tends to be a good predictor of their preference, even if they speak unofficially. Latin Americans tend to blame international events beyond their control. Industrial-country officials and commercial bankers tend to focus on errors made by Latin Americans. Academics are most inclined to cite both factors, although their political leanings may color the intensity of their insistence on where reforms are most needed.

Manuel Azpúrua, Venezuelan minister of finance, acknowledged that Latin American countries bore some responsibility for the current crisis. They had borrowed to finance investment projects that were not economically justifiable and to cover "nonproductive governmental expenditures." But Azpúrua chose to underline that it was the "excess of liquidity" in the international capital markets that allowed developing countries to borrow more than they could absorb efficiently. Having accumulated large debts bearing adjustable interest rates, the Latin American nations suddenly found their debt payments soaring way beyond what they had anticipated. Latin America's predicament was further exacerbated when the commercial banks then reversed field and decided that the continent was a bad credit risk. Given that the Latin Americans had grown accustomed to financing a good portion of their debt payments with new loans, the banks' retrenchment severely worsened the debtor nations' financial position.

Azpúrua noted that Latin American nations during the period from 1982 through 1985 have transferred some $106 billion in net resources to the international financial system; that is, payments on interest and profit remittances now vastly exceed net new lending. This drain represents a sharp departure from the previous norm, in which the industrial nations transferred resources to capital-poor developing countries. This resource transfer from South to North also amounts to a massive drain on Latin American resources, accounting for about 5 percent of GDP and 25 percent or more of domestic savings in many countries.

Jésus Silva-Herzog, Mexican finance minister, argued that "all parties were responsible for recycling petrodollars" and for the buildup of debt. The responsibility of the current predicament was "shared." He might have added that "the theory of the three s's" was superficial. Those who claim that "stupid loans were made by stupid banks to stupid countries" miss the point. When the loans were made, lenders and borrowers alike made assumptions, not unreasonable at the time, that anticipated that the Latin American nations could expand their exports rapidly enough to service the debt. How were they to predict that OPEC should again hike oil prices in 1979 and 1980, that the industrial countries would choose to fight inflation with tight money, that a Republican administration in the United States would run a loose fiscal policy that would put upward pressure on interest rates, that commodity prices would remain sluggish in the midst of a global recovery . . . in short, that the world of the 1980s would look dramatically different than the world of the 1970s? Thus, loans that looked reasonably good at the outset were transformed into bad credits by large unforeseeable events beyond the control of either lenders or borrowers.

Eduardo Wiesner, the western hemisphere director of the International Monetary Fund, and Pedro-Pablo Kuczynski, co-chairman, First Boston International, both noted that the current retrenchment by the commercial banks was damaging the prospects for recovery in Latin America and that international economic developments had important implications for Latin America. However, both emphasized the domestic policies of Latin American nations as the cause of the current crisis *and* the route to future growth. Wiesner identified the fiscal policies of Latin American governments as "the most important factor behind the insurgence of the debt crisis." Expansionary fiscal policies generated a demand for external borrowing. Fiscal deficits also squeezed the private sector by absorbing domestic financial resources and caused inflation by forcing governments to run the printing presses.

Kuczynski directly criticized the development model followed by Latin American nations, particularly the excessive growth of the public sector and the lack of export orientation. He noted that spending and borrowing by the public sector in many countries had risen dramatically, thereby crowding out the private sector. Latin American firms outside Brazil had paid insufficient attention to export markets in part because they enjoyed protected markets at home. But Kuczynski did not limit his critique to governments; he also denounced the "concessionaire style of private enterprise," where firms enjoyed oligopolistic positions and received handsome subsidies and official protection. These coddled businesses were not competitive on international markets, and they also tended to block internal reforms that threatened their privileged status. However, Kuczynski did hold out hope for the future, noting the recent emergence of a new generation of entrepreneurs and public servants, many educated in the United States, that understood the need for a more dynamic private sector oriented toward international markets.

Albert Fishlow, a professor of economics at the University of California in Berkeley, emphasized the external factors behind the debt crisis. In particular, Fishlow rebutted those who argue that external borrowing merely replaced domestic savings, noting that investment rates rose throughout most of Latin America during the 1970s. He also differed with those who maintain that most of the borrowed funds were wasted, drawing attention to the solid growth rates achieved by many countries. In short, Latin American economies "are not basket cases." Fishlow also countered the view that a very large portion of the borrowed money was diverted into capital flight and estimated that only about 20 percent of the $400 billion in capital inflows was transferred out of the region.

The Costs of the Debt Crisis

The various discussants left little doubt that the debt crisis has spread its damage very widely, thereby adversely affecting a diverse set of economic and political interests in Latin America and the United States. Participants differed, however, as to which interests had suffered most intensely and whether the burden of adjustment had been shared equitably.

Jimmy Carter reported that during a recent visit to several Latin American countries he became aware of the depth of preoccupation in the region with the debt problem. He also noted that debt was obstructing progress on other issues, including human rights and democracy. Carter remarked that the U.S. population tended, mistakenly, to see debt as a distant problem and failed to realize that it was impinging on vital U.S. interests. He noted the loss of jobs in U.S. export industries because depressed Latin American economies had to cut back purchases of U.S. products. Carter also suggested that U.S. foreign assistance efforts were defeated by a debt burden, which consumed U.S. aid. U.S. aid flows to Costa Rica, for example, were diverted to servicing that nation's foreign debt, and, in effect, never left the United States.

Howard Baker underscored the costs of the crisis to the United States. The U.S. economy was suffering from the loss of jobs in the export sector, and the assets of U.S. banks were at risk. Most importantly, U.S. strategic interests were at stake because regional democracy and political stability were threatened.

Senator Bill Bradley emphasized with great force the costs to U.S. workers, calling them "the unacknowledged victims of the debt crisis." The decline in U.S. exports to Latin America has resulted in the loss of more than 1 million jobs, adding half a percentage point to the U.S. unemployment rate. U.S. firms also have paid—from 1981 to 1983, U.S. exports of machinery fell by 38 percent, of steel and motor vehicles by 50 percent, and of agricultural machinery by more than 85 percent. In short, "U.S. workers and farmers have lost jobs and markets while banks have continued to profit from Latin American loans." Bradley perceived a conflict of interests between U.S. banks and U.S. farmers and manufacturers and found that the debt strategies pursued to date had benefited U.S. financial interests to the detriment of U.S. producers. Bradley concluded that "the economic security of millions of Americans requires a better deal."

Bradley also noted that the debt crisis had a perceptible impact on the U.S. trade position. Between 1981 and 1984, the annual U.S. trade deficit with Latin America had increased by $23 billion, which exceeded the $18 billion increase with Japan. In addition, the decline in U.S. production also meant that many firms were paying lower taxes, thereby exacerbating the U.S. fiscal deficit.

Terence C. Canavan, executive vice president, Chemical Bank, did not attempt to weigh the relative costs being borne by different interests. Instead he argued that it was erroneous to believe that the banks had gotten off scot-free. In fact, the banks were absorbing losses in several respects. Banks had taken some direct losses, principally on loans to private firms in Latin America, and also were selling some loans at a discount to nonbanks. Canavan estimated losses from these two processes at $4 billion. Furthermore, banks were paying "opportunity costs" on money tied up in forced rescheduling, and that were unavailable for potentially more profitable investment. Bank stocks had declined as a result of the erosion of confidence in future bank earnings, making it more costly to raise new equity. Government regulations had added to the banks' burdens by requiring larger reserves and reduced asset-to-capital ratios, both of which cut into bank profitability.

Silva-Herzog argued forcibly that Latin American economies have paid dearly—and unfairly. "The shared responsibility for the origins of the problem has been avoided. We have muddled through, but the costs have been high and unequally shared." He remarked that whereas Latin America had paid more than $100 billion in interest from 1982 to 1985, the region had received only $18 billion in new loans and investment. The banks, it is true, had reduced their "spread," or profit margins, but "only modestly." The terms of trade also have turned against Latin America, resulting in a substantial decrease in export earnings for some countries. The fall in the price of oil may cost Mexico $7 billion in 1986. (Although Silva-Herzog does not state it explicitly, it is clear that non-oil producing states in Latin America and U.S. consumers have benefited in terms of trade at the expense of Latin American oil producers.)

In order to generate the foreign exchange needed to service the debt, Latin America had to reduce its imports, which included slashing purchases by government and private consumers. Latin American imports were slashed from $98 billion in 1981 to less than $60 billion in 1985—far in excess of what many observers originally thought either politically or economically feasible. Per capita income levels fell by 9 percent between 1980 and 1985; excluding the relatively high growth cases of Brazil and Cuba, in the average Latin American country personal incomes dropped 11 percent.

Silva-Herzog expressed the fear that Latin America was now caught in a downward cycle, in a self-fulfilling prophecy. Having lost confidence in the region, creditors and investors were unwilling to risk their capital—thereby depriving the region of the means for breaking out of a low-growth debt trap. Although Latin America admittedly needed to raise its own savings rates, it still needed to receive foreign savings to resume satisfactory growth rates.

Gus Speth, president of the World Resources Institute, argued that the debt crisis has had a negative impact on efforts in debtor countries to prevent environmental degradation and improve the management of their natural resources. He noted that some "contradictory forces were at work" and that the capital shortage had forced a closer look at the sort of large capital-incentive projects that had caused such environmental damage in the past. He might have added that economic downturns had reduced the demand for energy and that lower levels of economic activity meant less industrial pollution. On the other hand, Speth warned that there is a widespread belief, supported by some mainly anecdotal evidence, that "the debt crisis is slowly undermining hard-fought recent gains in resource conservation and environmental protection." Austerity measures and economic stress have caused governments to cut environmental agencies and programs and to pay less attention to environmental issues. Speth also noted that the financial crisis had put pressure on developing countries to expand agricultural production and exports; Speth expressed concern that the result would be deforestation and increased land concentration, with the marginalized poor migrating to less fertile, erosion-prone lands.

Debate among the participants concentrated on the distribution of the costs of adjustment between North and South—that is, between industrialized and developing countries—but the discussion also covered the distribution of the burden among conflicting interest groups within both industrial and developing countries. Bill Bradley addressed the distributional issue in the context of competing U.S. interests, while Fishlow outlined the distribution of costs within the South. Fishlow noted that inequality had worsened in Latin America during the 1980s primarily as a result of two factors: the sharp decline in wages, which of course hurt workers, and the sharp increase in interest rates, which most directly benefited savers and therefore more affluent individuals. He might have added that capital flight also benefited its middle- and upper-class practitioners by protecting their assets against the massive devaluations experienced by many Latin American currencies since the debt crisis began in 1982. Although the panelists did not have time to enter into in-depth, statistical analysis of income distribution trends, it did appear that workers had fared badly in both the United States and Latin America.

Several speakers warned that the debt crisis was a potential threat to Latin American democracy. To date, the debt crisis actually had permitted democracy; the many authoritarian regimes that were in power during the beginning of the debt crisis suffered severe losses of popularity. But several speakers questioned the survivability of democratic institutions if economic austerity persists. Daniel Oduber, former president of Costa Rica, noted that democracy must have a social content and that if rising expectations of better living standards are not met, democracy might perish. Similarly, Bill

Bradley warned that "democracy cannot take root and flourish without the tangible promise of a better life."

Progress So Far and Problems that Remain

Since 1982 all parties to the debt crisis have been struggling to adjust to new conditions. These efforts have not been fruitless, and considerable progress has been made in improving the external balances of Latin American nations, restructuring outstanding debts, improving the balance sheets of the banks, and strengthening the international financial institutions charged with managing debt and development. Nevertheless, all the participants agreed that the debt issue was still pressing and that serious problems remained. Some speakers expressed concern about the omnipresent risks of an eventual confrontation between debtors and creditors, or of a collapse of the current debt strategy due to a deterioration of the international economy or to political instability in debtor nations.

Eduardo Wiesner presented the most optimistic assessment of progress to date, particularly during 1983 and 1984. For Latin America as a whole the current account deficit was reduced from an annual average of $43 billion in 1981 and 1982 to less than $10 billion in 1984 and 1985. The three largest countries—Argentina, Brazil, and Mexico—moved from a combined current account deficit of $30 billion in 1981 to a small surplus in 1984. Wiesner attributed much of this progress to improvements in fiscal accounts and noted that several countries had sliced in half their public sector deficits as a percentage of GDP. It should be noted, however, that these improvements in financial balances were attained largely by reducing imports and expenditures and by lowering the levels of commerce and consumption.

William Rhodes, vice president, Citibank, described three phases of the debt crisis. During the first phase in 1982 and 1983, the banks massively rescheduled debts and extended some loans, generally in conjunction with financial packages arranged by the International Monetary Fund. During the second phase, the banks negotiated multiyear restructuring arrangements to several countries, including Mexico, Venezuela, the Dominican Republic, Ecuador, Uruguay, and Yugoslavia. Now, during the third phase, banks should return gradually to "voluntary lending with a push," as countries regain their creditworthiness. The days of large-scale syndicated loans are past, and the banks now are more likely to extend project and trade finance and to enter into co-financing arrangements with official agencies.

Although the point was not discussed at any length during the conference, it also is true that the banks have been adjusting their own balance sheets to reduce their vulnerability to Latin American debtors. When the debt crisis first hit, the banks found their exposure to be an alarming multiple of their capital—nine major banks had loans outstanding to Mexico and Brazil alone that nearly equaled their total capital. Banks have been working hard to hold down new loans while building up their primary capital, including loan loss reserves. U.S. banks have succeeded in lowering their exposure in developing countries, as a percentage of their capital, from a peak of 186 percent in 1982 to 141 percent by the end of 1984; the ratio for Latin American countries dropped from about 120 percent to 93 percent. The major banks are more exposed but also have been making progress. For the nine largest U.S. banks, including Citibank and Chemical, the ratio of loans to developing countries in relation to their capital has fallen from 288 percent to 224 percent and for Latin America from 177 percent to 146 percent.

The global economy also has made progress. Terence C. Canavan, Eduardo Wiesner, and David C. Mulford, assistant secretary for international affairs of the U.S. Treasury Department, all emphasized that the recovery in industrial country growth, lower interest rates, falling oil prices, and expanding world trade created an environment more conducive to Latin American growth. Not surprisingly, Jésus Silva-Herzog and Manuel Azpúrua noted that the drop in oil prices adversely affected Mexico and Venezuela, but Mulford countered that oil exporters will enjoy some indirect benefits from fallen oil prices, including the higher rates of OECD growth, lower interest rates, and more buoyant export markets for non-oil exports.

C. Fred Bergsten, director of the Institute for International Economics, conceded that recent initiatives by the Group of Five leading industrial countries to lower the dollar were valuable, but should not be merely ad hoc actions. Moreover, cooperation should be expanded to encompass national macroeconomic policies, so as to ensure balanced, sustained global growth.

The Bretton Woods institutions—the IMF and World Bank—also have responded to the debt crisis. As Eduardo Wiesner pointed out, IMF disbursements to Latin America rose from negligible levels in 1981 to $6.6 billion in 1983, accounting for nearly half of total disbursements. The IMF was able to take a leadership role in managing the debt crisis because the Reagan administration decided to reverse its earlier opposition to an increase in IMF resources. Initially, some political appointees in the U.S. Treasury Department feared that a large quota increase might result in less rigorous conditionality and might transform the IMF from a short-term lender of last resort into a development agency. But concern that private capital markets were near collapse drove the Reagan administration to support an accelerated and substantial increase in quotas. As a result, IMF resources were increased in 1983 by 47.5 percent, to SDR 90 billion, and the IMF's General Arrangements to Borrow were boosted from approximately SDR 6.4 billion to SDR 17 billion. This roughly doubled the resources potentially available to the IMF.

The IMF recognized that even these augmented resources were insufficient to stabilize financial markets and that if all banks ceased lending at once, many might perish in the ensuing financial panic and contraction. The IMF also was concerned not to appear merely to be bailing out private banks. It therefore worked with the U.S. government to block the banks' flight from the Third World by conditioning its loans on agreements by the commercial banks to participate in financial packages for countries accepting IMF stabilization programs. The debt crisis thrust the IMF into a very powerful role, making it the single largest source of new funds for debtor countries as well as the central coordinator for private and even some other official flows.

Although not represented among the conference speakers, the World Bank is playing an increasingly important role in international finance. The World Bank was slow to respond to the debt crisis, taking a back seat to the IMF during 1982-1984. More recently, the World Bank has striven to increase both the volume and impact of its lending, to play a greater role in catalyzing private flows, and to regain some of the influence lost to the IMF. The loan commitments of the nonconcessional window, the International Bank for Reconstruction and Development (IBRD), rose from $9.8 billion in 1982 to $13.1 billion in 1985, and gross disbursements rose from $6.7 billion to $8.4 billion. Latin America shared in these increases, with disbursements rising from $2 billion to $3.1 billion. Nevertheless, if the World Bank is to play a greater role in managing the problems of debt and development, it clearly will need more resources; the increased expenditures in recent years were significant in percentage terms but amounted to only a tiny increment compared to the debtor nations' financial needs. Bank management would like to have the capacity to expand IBRD annual lending to $21.5 billion (compared to $11.5 billion in FY 1985), a goal requiring that the World Bank's authorized capital of $78.5 billion be increased by about $53 billion.

The increased efforts by the IMF and World Bank have been insufficient to offset the retrenchment of the commercial banks. Net annual private lending fell by a spectacular $37 billion between 1980-1982 and 1983-1985, while average annual net disbursements by the multilateral agencies rose by less than $5 billion. The countercyclical measures of official agencies have fallen short. Whereas their loan levels have risen significantly in relation to their own past performance, the increased flows have compensated for only a small percentage of the blows registered by the commercial markets.

Eduardo Wiesner lamented the banks' unwillingness to lend: "Although it was desirable that the private international banks reduce the increases in their exposure from the unsustainable rates during the period 1978 to 1981, the extent to which their lending has slowed down now poses a major problem." He warned that the lack of external resources constitutes a serious threat to the efforts of Latin American nations to reform their economies. Jesus Silva-Herzog added that developing countries have continued to service their debts in the hope that "good behavior" would stimulate renewed lending. The frustration of these hopes now was weakening their original resolve to service the debt.

Even those speakers who underscored the advances registered since 1982 recognized that serious problems and uncertainties remain in three key areas: the international economy, resource availability, and Latin American economic policies. Would the international economy provide the steady growth, open markets, and lower interest rates that are necessary if not sufficient conditions for Latin America to grow its way out of debt? Would the official lending agencies and the commercial banks provide Latin America with the resources needed to fund new investments while allowing for gradually increasing levels of per capita consumption? Would the Latin American nations use the available resources wisely and undertake the radical structural adjustments necessary to accommodate their economies to the new international realities?

Solutions

All of the contributors offered recommendations for future policy. The dominant subject was the size of anticipated and necessary capital flows, and participants differed markedly regarding desirable amounts and modalities of future resource transfers. Important disagreements also surfaced in debates regarding the development strategies that Latin America ought to follow and the best means for encouraging them. Greater harmony reigned during discussions of the international economy and how it could best foster adjustment and growth in Latin America.

David C. Mulford reiterated that the U.S. debt initiative, known as the Baker Plan, provided for increased financing from the commercial banks and the international financial institutions. The Baker Plan, proposed by Secretary of the Treasury James A. Baker III in Seoul, Korea, in October 1985, called on the World Bank and the Inter-American Development Bank to increase their disbursements to principle debtors by roughly 50 percent during a three-year period from the current level of nearly $6 billion, or by a total of $9 billion, while the commercial banks would provide $20 billion in net lending during the same three years, for a total package of $29 billion. Mulford chose to underscore the need for the IMF to continue playing a strong role, concentrating its resources in relatively short-term balance-of-payments problems, while the World Bank would provide fast-disbursing sectoral and structural adjustment loans. Mulford said that the World Bank has ample capacity to increase such lending by $2 billion per year during the next three years. He added that "we also are prepared, if all the participants in the [Baker Plan] strategy do their part and there is a demonstrated increase in the demand for quality lending in excess of these levels, to consider a general capital increase for the World Bank."

C. Fred Bergsten and Albert Fishlow both countered by arguing that about $20 billion per year was needed by the principal debtors—not the $10 billion provided for in the Baker Plan. Fishlow said the $10 billion might buy balance-of-payments adjustment, while another $10 billion was needed for growth—an objective to which the Baker Plan had given highest priority. This extra $10 billion might make the difference between 3 percent and 5 percent annual growth and would permit debtors to liberalize their trade regimes and increase imports—prerequisites for investment and export promotion. Bergsten suggested several possible sources for increased finance—a more aggressive World Bank could increase lending $4-5 billion if granted a substantial general capital increase of 50-100 percent of authorized capital and if the World Bank transferred some of its $20 billion in liquid holdings to worthy developing nations; the IMF could issue $10-15 billion in Special Drawing Rights (SDRs) per year for three years; industrial-country export credit agencies could be more forthcoming; and new sources of capital, such as pension and mutual funds, could be tapped. Both Bergsten and Fishlow emphasized the importance of making capital available rapidly to relieve current financial constraints and to support governments undertaking crucial structural reforms. At the same time, Fishlow urged lenders to undertake multiyear commitments in order to allow governments to engage in medium-term planning.

Pedro-Pablo Kuczynski argued that the existing financial situation was not sustainable and that Latin America could not be expected to continue generating a trade surplus of about 4 percent of GDP in order to service its debts. He argued that net capital inflows equivalent to 2-3 percent of Latin America's GDP were necessary in order to reduce the capital drain.

In response, Mulford queried: "Where should more money beyond the [Baker Plan's] $10 billion per year come from?" Gramm-Rudman makes it very difficult to ask Congress for new funds, and any new expenditures would be likely to give priority to U.S. farmers and energy-producing regions in the United States. The commercial banks are unwilling to extend more loans, and the developing countries themselves are hesitant to borrow more. The World Bank must maintain the quality of its loan portfolio. He added that new private investment would be welcome, and governments should work to convince their citizens to repatriate flight capital.

Bergsten suggested that the World Bank act as a "ringmaster" to pull the Bank, the IMF, and the commercial banks together, to link increased official and private financing with policy reform in the debtor nations. The IMF had played a similar role during the first phase of the debt crisis in 1982 and 1983. Silva-Herzog also endorsed the concept of close cooperation between the international financial agencies and the private banks. Terence Canavan warned against governmental control of lending in the long term.

Canavan said that the commercial banks had endorsed the Baker Plan and would be willing to lend when and if the other "legs" of the plan were in place, including the IMF and World Bank programs in support of economic reforms. The debtor nations had to create an environment in which the banks "can enter and exit." Debt can then increase, although "[one hopes] at a slower pace than GNP."

Mulford introduced the problem of capital flight, noting that it had been equivalent to virtually all new bank lending to Latin America in recent years. Kuczynski considered flight capital to be a potentially important source of capital inflows—provided that nations could undertake and sustain proper policy reforms. Silva-Herzog remarked that stable growth was the best incentive for capital repatriation but that the commercial banks also might refrain from promoting capital flight. He also maintained that the degree of capital flight from his country had been exaggerated, that Mexican deposits in U.S. banks amounted to about $14 billion, having increased by only $3 billion between 1983 and 1985.

While expressing his support for continued lending to debtor nations, Silva-Herzog also suggested that there was a need for "interest-rate relief." Bill Bradley went a step further and emphasized debt relief as an alternative to new commercial loans:

> In the long run, the U.S. national interest, the interest of the inter-American community, and the stability of the international financial system all depend on making the debt burden bearable. New lending is becoming politically intolerable in Latin America and is threatening the stability of money center banks, which continue to have inadequate capital to cover new Latin American exposure. Enormous interest/export ratios of close to 50 percent are discouraging new investment in Latin America. Yet the Baker Plan misguidedly calls for still more new loans, not less.

Bradley called for the formation of a seven-member council to coordinate the actions of commercial creditors, their governments, and the multilateral lending agencies. The council would evaluate debtor-country economic plans and offer a package of debt relief options appropriate to those plans. The council would be assisted by a panel of experts who might propose "temporary interest rate relief, relief on official loans, and loans from the World Bank for projects that can be completed quickly." A regulatory review board also should be established to prevent tax and accounting habits from forestalling a solution to the crisis.

Bergsten criticized Bradley's proposal on the grounds that he failed to specify who would pay for debt relief; Bergsten also questioned the need for new committees. He expressed hope that the World Bank could fill the existing policy void with its new president, Barber Conable. Coming to Bradley's defense, Jimmy Carter suggested that Bradley was appropriately worried about who would get us all going again and about the chronic net capital outflow draining Latin America.

Economic Reforms

The conferees agreed that regardless of the external financial situation, the Latin American nations needed to make major changes in their economic policies. Eduardo Wiesner suggested that the key to future growth lay in three policy areas: increasing domestic savings, increasing public-sector efficiency, and increasing exports and liberalizing foreign trade. Mulford argued along similar lines for tax reform, privatization of public enterprises, development of more efficient domestic capital and equity markets, improvement in the environment for investment, and trade liberalization. Mulford recognized that such reforms can be politically difficult, although he pointed to the recent experiences in Brazil and Argentina to suggest that reforms also can be popular.

Silva-Herzog conceded that domestic reform was needed in many debtor nations. Developing countries have to become more export oriented and more internationally competitive. But he cautioned that we must be careful in the application of recipes for structural change. Mulford agreed that the United States should not dictate conditionality, a task better left to the IMF and World Bank, and that reform strategies should come mostly from within the developing countries that have to implement them.

Bradley was most critical of the current mechanisms for initiating policy reform in Latin America. He denounced policies that are imposed from abroad and that have a strong ideological bias oriented toward reducing wages and shrinking the public sector as "a kind of supply-side imperialism." Instead, he called for the substitution of "partnership" for "conditionality" and urged that "Latin American initiative, not supply-side dogmatism, [be] the basis of a strategy for sustainable growth."

Fishlow took a middle position on conditionality. He urged caution and noted that finance ministers in Latin America have become more political and national presidents more economically sophisticated. He also reminded the audience that recent reforms in Brazil and Argentina were indigenously devised and went beyond typical IMF proposals. With regard to the content of reform, Fishlow agreed with those speakers who called for export growth and for stronger private sectors, but with important qualifications. He called for an "export-adequate" strategy that combines export growth with an expansion of the domestic market as Brazil had accomplished. Essentially, export growth should keep pace with GNP growth. He advocated better cooperation between the public and private sectors and called for efforts, within budgetary constraints, to correct the economic inequalities that had worsened during the 1980s.

All the conferees agreed that Latin America could overcome its twin problems of debt and development only if the industrial countries provided a supportive environment of steady, sustained global growth, moderate interest rates, and open trading markets. Thus, all the parties to the problem—the industrial nations, the Latin Americans, the commercial banks, the international financial institutions—have important responsibilities in helping to resolve the hemisphere's greatest economic crisis since the 1930s.

chapter fifteen

Planning for the Future

Robert A. Pastor

Robert J. Samuelson, the economist who writes columns for *Newsweek*, offered a pungent but perplexing synopsis of the debt crisis from the U.S. perspective: "Latin countries are impoverishing themselves so that we can enjoy higher unemployment and protectionist pressures. They have had to export more and import less to generate trade surpluses in dollars to repay dollar debts."[1]

Why have Latin America and the United States permitted the crisis to continue for so long with such mutually negative consequences? The answer is not the absence of ideas. This book contains numerous proposals, and there are many others already in the public domain. This chapter summarizes and organizes these proposals. I then try to explain why these solutions have not been chosen, but why they might be in the future.

Essentially, there are two broadly defined strategies for addressing the debt crisis: a financial strategy and a development strategy. They are not necessarily mutually exclusive; elements of both can be, and have been, combined. But for the moment, let us treat them separately.

A Financial Strategy

The financial strategy has treated the debt crisis largely as a temporary liquidity problem. The objective has been to help debtors pay their debts and to assure the stability of the international financial system. The premise of this strategy is that world growth will ameliorate and eventually eliminate the debt problem. Therefore, costly long-term proposals ought to be avoided.

The IMF has been the principal executor of this strategy, formulating adjustment strategies for the debtor countries and making standby loans. The banks have played important roles rescheduling debts and lending sufficient new funds to permit the debtors to pay the interest on the old debts. When the strategy proved inadequate in 1985, Secretary Baker offered a plan based on the same principles, but with more resources and coordination between the various actors.

The Baker Plan, an improved variant of the financial strategy, was first tested on Mexico, but whether it passed the test is debatable. Although there were fifteen eligible debtor nations, Mexico received nearly one-half of all resources promised by the Baker Plan, and it took seventeen months after the Plan was announced for Mexico to reach agreement with the banks. To continue to pay its debt, Mexico was compelled to accumulate an additional $12 billion. It is hard to envisage a better illustration of a postponement of the problem.

It would be incorrect to suggest that the current financial strategy has not been inventive; it has incorporated a number of new ideas. To strengthen the private sector in the developing world, for example, the Reagan administration has promoted several initiatives by the International Finance Corporation (IFC) of the World Bank. The IFC already has increased its role in development, pledging to invest $7.4 billion in more than four hundred projects from 1986 through 1990.

Three steps also have been taken to promote more private investment. First, a multilateral investment guaranty agency was established to ensure investors against commercial risks such as war or expropriation. Second, a mutual fund was established by the IFC to invest in securities in Third World countries. Third, the IFC established a program that will provide investors a guarantee against loss. By this program, an investor could receive the full amount of his or her capital at the end of ten or twenty years, but he or she also must be prepared to share dividend income and capital gains with the IFC and pay an origination fee.[2]

Besides the excellent critique of the Baker Plan in the chapter by Albert Fishlow, there are three other problems with the financial strategy. First, the strategy underestimates the long-term costs of the debt problem, including the effects of declining investment in infrastructure, education, health, and agriculture in Latin America. Second, if the world economy deteriorates, the time previously spent imposing austerity on these countries will have been wasted, the debt will not be repaid, and the shock to the international system will still be severe.

The third problem is the inverse of the second—although there have been a number of positive developments in the world economy since the onset of the crisis, the debt problem remains as serious as before, and Latin

America shows few, if any, signs of being able to recover from it. After being virtually stagnant in 1981 and 1982, world economic growth resumed—albeit at a more moderate pace—in 1983. The annual growth in world output rose to 4.4 percent in 1984, before dropping to 3.1 percent in 1985 and 2.9 percent in 1986.[3] The nominal interest rates—while still high by historical standards—declined by 50 percent from 1981 to 1986.[4] Oil prices, which dropped so precipitously from more than $30 a barrel in November 1985 to less than $12 a barrel by April 1986, recovered somewhat to about $18 a barrel a year later. As Eduardo Wiesner wrote, the International Monetary Fund—and other multilateral banks—expanded their resources since the onset of the crisis and have used them to keep the international financial system from collapsing.

Several of the authors in this book commented on Brazil's rapid growth and relative success in managing its heavy debt burden; but by late 1986, Brazil's Cruzado Plan, heralded as an alternative to IMF-imposed austerity, was relaxed for a moment, and the result was a burst of inflation. By the end of 1986, Brazil's trade surplus had deteriorated, the country's reserves declined by $5 billion, and Brazil sought $2 to 3 billion in new credits and a restructuring of its debt.[5] On February 20, 1987, Brazil unilaterally suspended interest payments.

In brief, despite some positive signs in the world economy and a moderately helpful response by elements in the international community, the persistent weight of debt service, the continuing growth in the debt, and the deterioration in the terms of trade have precluded the long-term recovery and development of *any* nation in Latin America—even Brazil. The financial strategy at best has been inadequate. Let me therefore summarize some of the longer-term solutions.

Long-Term Development Solutions

A development approach to the debt crisis views the issue as how to promote the long-term economic development of the region rather than how to permit Latin America to continue paying its debt. No serious political leader is proposing the repudiation or default of the entire debt; that would be too costly for all parties. But an increasing number of leaders have come to recognize that the only way that much of the debt could be repaid is if Latin America could shift its scarce resources toward domestic investment rather than debt service. The increase in investment in Latin America would also contribute to an invigoration of the international economic system.

To a certain extent, the distinction between a financial and a development strategy is a question of degree or, rather, of amount of money. To prevent default and permit balance-of-payments adjustments in Latin America, the region needs a total of $20 billion for a three-year period. However, according to both Albert Fishlow and Fred Bergsten, Latin America would need about $20 billion *each year* to attain a 4 percent annual rate of growth.

A long-term development solution would not just focus on national macroeconomic policies and the resources needed to attain certain objectives; it also would address issues related to regional integration. With the Marshall Plan, the United States offered Europe $17 billion during a four-year period, contingent on the Europeans agreeing to a single unified strategy for economic development and cooperation. This core concept of the Marshall Plan is relevant to Latin America's debt crisis and other problems as well.[6]

Instead of negotiating debt reschedulings on a case-by-case basis, the United States, the banks, and the international institutions ought to pledge an amount comparable to the Marshall Plan with the same kind of condition: Latin America would have to agree to lower its internal and external trade and investment barriers and develop a plan that would use the money for the benefit of the entire region rather than just for the benefit of each nation. The plan would need to benefit the region's poor, not just its rich. Increased funding for Latin America's growth would redound to the economic benefit of the United States much as the Marshall Plan did.

As one of the greatest foreign policy successes of the United States, the Marshall Plan, or rather variations of the plan, frequently are proposed to deal with crises of the moment. The Alliance for Progress, launched by President John Kennedy in 1961, originally was described as a Marshall Plan for Latin America, but economists soon recognized that the problem of Latin America in the 1960s was one of development whereas Europe's problem in the 1940s was one of economic recovery. By the 1980s, Latin America's economy resembled Europe's in the 1940s in terms of industrialization, skills, and infrastructure. What Latin America needs today is what Europe needed three decades before—a financial boost to facilitate recovery and further economic development. A U.N. study in November 1986 described the debt crisis as "the deepest and longest which the region has experienced in the last half century," but it also noted that the crisis should not "overshadow the fact that the stock of human, natural and capital resources, as well as the creative capacity of the population and the wide range of possibilities and situations which exist, represent a potential which, if properly developed, would enable this [developmental] challenge to be faced successfully."[7]

Bergsten recommended that the World Bank play the leading role in organizing and coordinating the long-term development response to the debt crisis. He also said that a doubling of the bank's capital would be needed if it were to play such a role. Kuczynski encouraged more lending for basic human needs and services—the long-term investments that have been neglected since the onset of the debt crisis.

Fishlow offered a number of innovative proposals. He suggested that Germany and Japan consider using their surplus capital like the OPEC nations did after they had accumulated similar surpluses: to establish an "oil facility" that could assist those nations that have been most severely affected by the change in the price of oil. This would be a "reverse oil facility."

Fishlow also recommended that the IMF Compensatory Financing Facility (CFF) be adapted so as to permit it to lend money if interest rates were to rise. The CFF currently lends money to countries that experience a shortfall in foreign exchange due to the decline in commodity prices. A rise in interest rates would affect developing countries much as would a decline in commodity prices, and the CFF could serve as a cushion if extended to this area. Finally, Fishlow proposed that the banks make multiyear financial commitments.

Speth explained that countries that divert capital from environmental management to debt service will not only mortgage their natural resource base, but they also will find it increasingly difficult to pay their debts. He offered five specific recommendations to promote long-term growth while at the same time improving the environment and natural resource management in debtor nations: (1) The IMF should give priority to preventing irreversible environmental and resource damage. (2) Part of the increased financing from the international development banks should aim to eliminate subsidies that encourage wasteful exploitation of forest, water, and energy resources. (3) New programs should be introduced to help developing countries upgrade their *own* environmental and resource management capabilities. (4) A larger portion of development assistance should be directed at improving the productivity of resource sectors, including forests and underutilized land. (5) Debts owed by the poorest countries should either be written off or be repaid in local currencies for small-scale agricultural or biological conservation projects.

No Latin American nation can sustain a long-term growth strategy as long as it exports 35 to 50 percent of its foreign exchange earnings each year in the form of debt service. Some form of debt relief is inescapable. Indeed, since 1982, the continual debt reschedulings can be viewed as one form of relief. However, the costs of the crisis have not been borne equitably, and the ad hoc approach has diverted attention and energy from long-term, development-oriented solutions.

Although it is now widely acknowledged that the responsibility for the debt crisis is a shared one between lenders and borrowers, the costs of the crisis have come to rest disproportionately on the developing nations as well as on the workers and industries of the industrialized nations. The trade-off is unequivocal: Latin American borrowers have had to reduce their imports from the United States to service their debts. There are many different estimates of the number of jobs that were lost or not created in the United States as a result of Latin America's reduced imports, but no one questions that the impact has been severe. Proposals to reduce Latin America's debt service burden would not only permit more investment in the region, but it would create jobs in the United States.[8]

The Joint Economic Committee estimated that a reduction of $12 billion in Latin America's debt service would correspond to an increase of $6 billion in U.S. exports to the region. It is true that the banks would pay for this reduction, but the Committee estimated that after-tax profits of U.S. banks would be reduced by only $1 billion, as compared to $3.4 billion of after-tax profits of the nine money-centered banks in 1985.[9] This would appear a small cost for the banks and a significant benefit for Latin America and U.S. industry.

A long-term arrangement on debt relief within the context of a comprehensive development plan for Latin America would not only permit a more equitable distribution of the costs of the crisis, but it would also provide security for the banks and a foundation for prosperity. The three methods for reducing debt service are: (1) limit debt service; (2) reduce payments on interest and/or principal; and (3) convert debt partially or totally into local currency, equity, or securities. There are numerous specific proposals for achieving each of these three objectives.

Senator Bill Bradley offered the boldest approach. Instead of trying to dictate to the Latin American debtors, Senator Bradley sought to elicit a plan from them, which could then be subject to discussions and negotiations involving all the key actors of the international community. This plan would not only focus on the nation's future growth but also on debt relief. Instead of new commercial loans, he recommended reducing the previous debt. Among the kinds of relief that he mentioned are temporary interest rate relief, relief on official loans, and quick-disbursing World Bank loans.

As a target for the total value of annual debt relief packages, Bradley recommended: (1) 3 points of interest rate relief for one year on all outstanding commercial and bilateral loans; (2) 3 percent write-down and forgiveness of principal on all outstanding commercial and bilateral loans to eligible countries; and (3) $3 billion of new multilateral project and structural adjustment loans for eligible countries. Bradley also suggested the establishment of a review board to recommend the modification of bank regulations and tax and accounting rules to allow debt restructuring.

There are many variations on Bradley's proposal as well as other ideas offered by some of the contributors to this volume.[10] Let me briefly outline some of them:

1. *Limit debt service*
   a. Oaxtepec Communiqué, Mexico, "Grow to Pay" recommended a formula to set a ceiling on debt payments to permit a minimum level of growth.
   b. The Peruvian Proposal set maximum rate of payment to 10 percent of export earnings.

2. *Reduce interest payments*
   a. The Cartagena Group, at its meeting in December 1985 in Montevideo, recommended reducing interest payments "to historical levels."
   b. Reduce commissions or fees.
   c. Automatically capitalize interest if interest rises above a predetermined ceiling.

3. *Reduce principal*
   a. Steve Hanke proposed that banks should be required periodically to "mark to the market" their loans to Latin American nations by valuing loans on their books according to the market value. In effect, this means that Latin loans would be written down and losses incurred. This would encourage banks to sell their loans at the market rate and also would permit some innovative approaches, including debt-for-equity swaps.[11]
   b. Changes in bank regulations could facilitate the expansion of secondary discount markets, which could reduce the size of the debt.

4. *Convert debt partially or totally*
   a. Víctor Urquidi proposed that Latin Americans pay part of their debt in local currency that would be put in special accounts held by banks and only be used to finance development projects mutually agreed upon by the debtor and creditor.[12]
   b. Either the banks or a purchaser of the bank's loans could sell the loan to the government in exchange for obtaining equity in a corporation or a specific project. (Chile has such a program.)[13]
   c. Bank assets also could be transferred to multilateral agencies at reduced prices in exchange for international guarantees. Three such options are:
      (1) Professor Peter Kenen proposed a new international debt discount corporation to buy up debt at a 10 percent discount and pay the banks in long-term bonds. That corporation would then grant the debtor nations reductions in interest payments and renegotiate the debt.[14]

(2) Felix Rohatyn proposed that the debt be stretched to long-term maturities of fifteen to thirty years and interest reduced to 6 percent. The schedule of payments would be limited to a maximum of 25-35 percent of exports annually. An international entity would buy the loans at a discount. Banks would sustain some loss, but they would gain greater security.[15]

(3) In general, a multilateral guarantee from an international institution would permit banks to reduce interest rates in return for greater security on some of the loans.

Just because the current "solutions" to the debt crisis are costly does not mean that one automatically embraces these alternatives. The issue is whether these alternatives cost more or less, and who pays? These proposals would transfer some of the burden of the debt crisis from the borrowing countries to the lending banks. In 1982, many of these banks were so exposed that a massive write-down would have shaken the U.S. banking system and very possibly the entire world economy. Today, all of the banks have reduced their exposure and increased their profit margins.

It is no longer impossible to contemplate some bank write-downs of their debts. In late 1986, Republic National Bank of New York became the first of Mexico's major lenders to write down a significant portion of its debt. This was the first time that a U.S. bank acknowledged by its action that it was not going to be paid. At the time, the market for Mexican government debt was roughly seventy cents on the dollar.[16]

After the suspension of interest payments by Brazil in February 1987, three major banks announced they would place their loans to Brazil on nonaccrual status, which meant that they would no longer record income when the interest on their loans were due. These banks therefore reduced their net income.[17]

Nonetheless, it remains difficult for either the banks or the U.S. government to contemplate across-the-board debt relief. In a letter sent to Senator Bradley on November 5, 1986, Federal Reserve Chairman Paul Volcker criticized Bradley's proposal because it would force banks to assume major losses that would harm the banking system and jeopardize future loans to Latin America. "In my judgment," Volcker wrote, "the short-term benefits of debt relief for a few debtor countries would be offset by the long-term adverse impact it would have on the supply of credit to all developing countries and, hence, on the health and vitality of the world economy."[18] Of course, one of the problems in the Baker Plan is that the major banks already have reduced or halted their lending to Latin America.[19]

In the letter, Volcker estimated that if 3 percent of the debt of the ten largest Latin American debtors were written off each year for three years and interest rates were reduced by 3 percent, the after-tax profits of the nine major U.S. banks would be reduced by about 50 percent of the level attained in 1985—$3.4 billion. Senator Bradley responded to the criticism by suggesting that the magnitude of the reduction in profits was probably exaggerated, but was still not excessive. Moreover, his plan did not call for debt forgiveness to all countries or in the same amount; only to those that accepted a plan examined and approved by an international group. Changes in bank regulations could facilitate write-downs by the banks while permitting future lending. The benefits of the plan would be in the way in which the capital that is used to service the debt could be used to invest in Latin America's development and purchase goods from the United States.

A variation on the Kenen proposal was implemented by twenty-eight Japanese banks that established a new company to purchase their loans to developing countries at a market-based discount. The total loan exposure in 1986 of these banks was $62 billion, about half as much as U.S. banks. The Japanese banks have a tax incentive to sell bad loans and move on to new opportunities. One analyst suggested that U.S. banks ought to adopt a similar formula and might do so if banking regulations and accounting rules were modified.[20]

To place these various proposals in perspective, it may be worth recalling that during the Great Depression, the debt principal owed by several European countries was reduced, and in 1953, the United States reduced Germany's debt from $3 billion to $1 billion and stretched it out to be repaid in thirty-five years at 3 percent interest. Although Latin America undoubtedly would welcome such an initiative today, the important point is that no Latin American nation has unilaterally taken such a step, which would be within its sovereign power. As important as that fact is the reason. Richard Fletcher, a former minister of planning of Jamaica, interpreted Latin America's motive:

> The responsible behavior of Latin American leadership is not due to lack of courage to confront the system. It is the product of a conviction that the international trading and financial system served Latin America well as it pursued economic development in the postwar period, and that it is in Latin America's long-term interest that this system persist and be strengthened, not weakened.[21]

Will

No single formula for resolving the debt crisis exists for every Latin American country. Any strategy needs to be adjusted to take into account the unique economic and financial situation of each country. Nonetheless, an overall solution to the debt problem should include the following five elements:

- An expanding world economy in which interest rates and barriers to trade decline
- A sharp increase—perhaps a doubling—of loans at below market rates from the multilateral development banks
- An increase in commercial bank lending and foreign direct investment
- Economic reforms to reduce fiscal deficits, increase domestic savings, and allocate the new capital into equitable development projects and productive ventures
- Debt restructuring and relief

There has been some movement in each of these areas, but not enough to deal effectively with the crisis. There has been almost no progress, however, on the pivotal question of debt relief, despite the proliferation of proposals. The problem is that every important proposal costs, and few are willing to pay. The banks fear that costly write-offs of the debt could jeopardize their own financial base. The United States is trying to reduce its own ballooning fiscal deficit, and Congress—with the exception of Senator Bill Bradley and a few others—appears unwilling to contemplate any proposal that might need government financing.[22] With the exception of Japan, the other industrialized countries have shown little inclination to address the problem, preferring the United States deal with it. The IMF and the World Bank are doing the best that limited resources permit.

The Latin American governments are not blameless. They have failed to exercise their leverage as a unified bloc. Instead of bargaining as the Cartagena Group or as a Latin American group, each country has split repeatedly from the others and sought the best deal it could get. Instead of demonstrating solidarity with Brazil when it suspended its interest payments in February 1987, Mexico, Argentina, Venezuela, and Chile took advantage of Brazil's distress and the banks' fears to negotiate agreements on new loans and rescheduling packages. The only Latin American leader who has genuinely sought a Latin American effort is Alan Garcia, but ironically, even he pursued his strategy unilaterally. Instead of gaining agreement from the region on his proposal to limit debt payments, he announced his proposal in his inaugural address. In the end, Latin America, too, has opted continually for a short-term fix rather than a long-term solution.

Richard Feinberg has summarized the state of the dialogue on the debt. There are many sensible and intelligent ideas but little will or imagination by the United States or the region's leadership to implement these. It is sometimes said that the world will have to suffer a terrible war before it makes the kinds of decisions necessary to establish a world government that could preclude such wars.

Similarly, and tragically, the world might have to await another global economic depression before it tackles the debt problem with the kind of vision and leadership embodied in the Marshall Plan. Although motivated by security concerns, the Marshall Plan's effect was to create and invigorate a new global economic system. Does the international community need a war or depression before it will take these far-sighted actions? The question for the inter-American community is whether the dialogue of the debt will remain a dialogue of the deaf or whether both sides will begin listening to each other and take steps that could transform the financial crisis into a global development opportunity. The issue is whether the inter-American community will continue adjusting to its past burden or whether it will begin planning for its future development.

Notes

1. Robert J. Samuelson, "How Do You Spell Relief?" *Newsweek,* October 21, 1985, p. 70.

2. Clyde H. Farnsworth, "Guarantee for Investors in Third World," *New York Times,* August 28, 1986, p. 33. For some innovative proposals for utilizing private investment in the Third World, see Theodore H. Moran (ed.), *Investing in Development: New Roles for Private Capital?* (New Brunswick, N.J.: Transaction Books for the Overseas Development Council, 1986).

3. International Monetary Fund, *World Economic Outlook* (Washington, D.C.: IMF, April 1987), Table A1, p. 117.

4. U.N. Economic Commission for Latin America and the Caribbean, *Latin American and Caribbean Development: Obstacles, Requirements and Options,* November 25, 1986, p. 101.

5. Alan Riding, "Brazilian Loan Request Is Expected," *New York Times,* January 12, 1986, p. 34.

6. For a proposal on how to apply the Marshall Plan to Central America and the Caribbean, see Robert Pastor and Richard Feinberg, "Latin America and the Marshall Plan Reflex," *Vital Issues* (Washington, Conn.: Center for Information on America, 1984).

7. U.N. Economic Commission for Latin America and the Caribbean, *Latin American and Caribbean Development: Obstacles, Requirements and Options,* November 1986, pp. vii-viii.

8. Stuart Tucker and Richard Feinberg of the Overseas Development Council estimated that the United States lost 632,000 jobs due to the decline in exports to the Third World between 1980 and 1985, and an additional 930,000 jobs would have been created during this period if the growth trend of the 1970s had continued. They also estimated the number of jobs that could be created if various debt relief pro-

posals were accepted. See the testimony of Richard E. Feinberg, "Third World Debt: Toward A More Balanced Adjustment," to the Subcommittee on International Debt of the Senate Finance Committee, March 9, 1987.

9. Joint Economic Committee of the Congress, *A Staff Study: The Impact of the Latin American Debt Crisis on the U.S. Economy,* May 10, 1986, pp. 36–39.

10. For specific proposals and analytical compendiums of proposals, see the following: C. Fred Bergsten, William R. Cline, and John Williamson, *Bank Lending to Developing Countries: The Policy Alternatives* (Washington, D.C.: Institute for International Economics, April 1985), especially pp. 60-66; Naciones Unidas, Comision Economica para America Latina y el Caribe, *Politicas de ajuste y renegociacion de la deuda externa en America Latina,* no. 48 (Santiago, 1984), especially p. 83; U.N. Economic Commission for Latin America and the Caribbean, *Latin American and Caribbean Development: Obstacles, Requirements and Options,* November 1986, pp. 98–108; and for one proposal, see Inter-American Dialogue, *Rebuilding Cooperation in the Americas* (Washington, D.C.: Aspen Institute, 1986), pp. 1–15.

11. Steven H. Hanke, "Forcing Banks to Mark Down Loans," *New York Times,* October 5, 1986, p. F3.

12. Víctor L. Urquidi, "A Proposal to Create a System for Part-Payment in Local Currency of Interest on External Debt" (Paper prepared at El Colegio de Mexico, February 1986).

13. For a discussion of these proposals, see Richard S. Weinert, "Swapping Third World Debt," *Foreign Policy* 65 (Winter 1986–87).

14. Peter B. Kenen, "Third World Debt: Sharing the Burden, A Bailout Plan for the Banks," *New York Times,* March 6, 1983.

15. See his testimony before the Senate Foreign Relations Committee, January 17, 1983.

16. Eric N. Berg, "Mexico Tie to Republic Write-Down," *New York Times,* January 15, 1987, pp. 29, 30.

17. Andrew Pollack, "Three Banks Reclassify Brazil Debt," *New York Times,* April 2, 1987, p. 29.

18. See letter to Senator Bill Bradley from Paul A. Volcker, November 5, 1986; Statement by Senator Bradley's office, January 20, 1987; and James L. Rowe, Jr., "Fed Casts Doubt on Bradley Plan," *Washington Post,* January 20, 1987, pp. C1, 3.

19. Baker himself acknowledged the seriousness of this problem. Clyde H. Farnsworth, "New Action on World Debt Urged: Baker Presses Banks to Keep Loans Flowing," *New York Times,* April 10, 1987, p. 29.

20. See Karin Lissakers, "A Lesson from Japanese Banks," *New York Times,* March 24, 1987, p. 27; and Eric N. Berg, "Japan Plan on Third World Debt," *New York Times,* March 6, 1987, p. 33.

21. Richard D. Fletcher, "Lessons of Recent Debt Reorganization," in *The Lingering Debt Crisis,* edited by Khadija Haq (Islamabad: North-South Roundtable, 1985), p. 100.

22. For another interesting proposal from Congress, see David R. Obey and Paul S. Sarbanes, "Recycling Surpluses to the Third World: A Marshall Plan for the 80's," *New York Times,* November 9, 1986. Obey was chairman of the Joint Economic Committee during the 99th Congress; and Sarbanes, for the 100th Congress beginning in January 1987.

The Baker Plan

Summary of a Statement by James A. Baker III, at the IMF/World Bank Annual Meeting, Seoul, South Korea, October 8, 1985

Sound policies and sustained low-inflation growth in the industrial countries must provide the essential foundation for a successful debt strategy, and are a prerequisite for stronger growth in the debtor countries.

A program for sustained growth incorporates three essential and mutually reinforcing elements: First and foremost, the adoption by principal debtor countries of comprehensive macroeconomic and structural policies, supported by the international financial institutions, to promote growth and balance of payments adjustment, and to reduce inflation. Second, a continued central role for the IMF, in conjunction with increased and more effective structural adjustment lending by the multilateral development banks (MDBs), both in support of the adoption by principal debtors of market-oriented policies for growth. Third, increased lending by the private banks in support of comprehensive economic adjustment programs.

The first part concerns the need for structural changes in the debtor countries, including: —increased reliance on the private sector, and less reliance on government, to help increase employment, production, and efficiency; —supply-side actions to mobilize domestic savings and facilitate efficient investment, both domestic and foreign, by means of tax reform, labor market reform, and development of financial markets; and—market-opening measures to encourage foreign direct investment and capital inflows, as well as to liberalize trade, including the reduction of export subsidies.

. . . This broader approach does not mean that policy areas that have been the focus of efforts to date—in particular fiscal, monetary, and exchange rate policies—can receive less attention. Indeed, macroeconomic policies have been central to efforts to date and must be strengthened to achieve greater progress. These policies should consist of: market-oriented exchange rate, interest rate, wage, and pricing policies to promote greater economic efficiency and responsiveness to growth and employment opportunities; and sound monetary and fiscal policies focused on reducing domestic imbalances and inflation and on freeing up resources for the private sector.

The cornerstone of sustained growth must be greater domestic savings, and investment of those savings at home. Macroeconomic and structural policies which improve economic efficiency, mobilize domestic resources, and provide incentives to work, save, and invest domestically will create the favorable economic environment necessary for this to occur. Such an environment is also critical to attract supplemental foreign savings.

As a practical matter, it is unrealistic to call upon the support of voluntary lending from abroad, whether public or private, when domestic funds are moving in the other direction. Capital flight must be reversed if there is to be any real prospect of additional funding, whether debt or equity. If a country's own citizens have no confidence in its economic system, how can others?

There are essentially two kinds of capital inflows: loans and equity investments. Foreign borrowings have to be repaid—with interest. Equity investment, on the other hand, has a degree of permanence and is not debt-creating. Moreover, it can have a compounding effect on growth, bring innovation and technology, and help to keep capital at home.

We believe that the debtor nations must be willing to commit themselves to these policies for growth in order that the other elements of a strengthened debt strategy can come into place.

There is ample room to expand the World Bank's fast-disbursing lending to support growth-oriented policies, and institutional and sectoral reform ... [but] emphasizing growth does not mean de-emphasizing the IMF. A serious effort to develop the programs of the World Bank and the Inter-American Development Bank (IDB) could increase their disbursements to principal debtors by roughly 50 percent from the current annual level of nearly $6 billion. ... It should be possible ... to streamline World Bank operations in order to reduce considerably the time period required to formulate and implement such assistance programs. This will expedite the actual disbursement of funds. ... The Bank should seek to assist, both in a technical and financial capacity, those countries which wish to "privatize" their state-owned enterprises, which in too many cases aggravate already serious budget deficit problems. ... There is also an urgent need for efforts to expand the Bank's cofinancing operations. The International Finance Corporation, with an expanded capital base, and the recently negotiated Multilateral Investment Guarantee Agency (MIGA) are two important Bank Group initiatives in support of developing countries. Both organizations can do much to assist their members in attracting non-debt capital flows as well as critical technological and managerial resources.

Our assessment of the commitment required by the banks to the entire group of heavily indebted, middle income developing countries would be net new lending in the range of $20 billion for the next three years. In addition, it would be necessary that countries now receiving adequate financing from banks on a voluntary basis continue to do so, provided they maintain sound policies. I would like to see the banking community make a pledge to provide these amounts of new lending and make it publicly, provided the debtor countries also make similar growth-oriented policy commitments as their part of the cooperative effort. Such financing could be used to meet both short-term financing and longer-term investment needs in the developing countries, and would be available, provided debtors took action and multilateral institutions also did their part. We would welcome suggestions from the banking community about arrangements which could be developed in order to ensure that adequate financing to support growth is available.

Latin America's Response: Excerpts from Communiqués of The Cartagena Group

Cartagena Consensus Document, June 22, 1984

A. They [the foreign and finance ministers of eleven Latin American nations with the largest debts—Argentina, Bolivia, Brazil, Chile, Colombia, Ecuador, Mexico, Peru, Dominican Republic, Uruguay, and Venezuela] pointed out that the region is undergoing an unprecedented crisis characterized by a severe decrease in the per capita product, which is now at the levels of a decade ago, and which has provoked an unemployment rate that already affects more than one-fourth of its economically active population and a substantial drop in real wages that could bring grave political and social consequences.

B. They stressed that to a great extent, the *crisis is due to external factors* outside the control of the Latin American countries, which from 1980 to 1983 provoked a decrease in exports and produced the forced contraction of imports with grave consequences for the development process. The international recession in that period, the stagnation of the economies of the industrialized countries, and the deterioration of the terms of trade and the re-emergence of restrictive and protectionist trade policies in the industrialized nations provoked grave retrogressions in the volume and structure of the exports of the region.

C. Those factors, along with the repeated increases in the interest rates, outline a grave and somber panorama of foreign indebtedness for the region's countries. The accumulated sum of Latin America's foreign debt is more than half of its gross internal product, or three times its annual exports. The debt service payments have registered an increase equivalent to almost double the increase of the exports, and in the last eight years the payment of interest represented more than $173 billion. Each percentage point that the interest rates increase represents for Latin America an additional expenditure of $2.5 billion a year in foreign exchange. The increase in the interest rates this year is equivalent to a month of exports of the region. The most negative result of this situation is that the region has become a net exporter of its financial resources. It is estimated that this loss amounted to approximately $30 billion in 1983. Paradoxically, while there are signs of economic recovery in most of the industrial countries, Latin America is forced to slow down and in some cases to paralyze its development process.

D. They stated that to a great extent the Latin American debt problem is due to drastic changes in the conditions in which the credits were originally contracted, especially with regard to the liquidity and the interest rates, the degree of participation of the multilateral credit organizations in the structure of the debt, and in the projects for economic growth. These changes show the joint responsibility of debtors and creditors.

E. They reiterated their intention to fulfill their pledges regarding their external debts. In no case will this mean disregarding their governments' duty to guarantee their peoples' welfare, and social and political stability.

F. They reaffirmed that these efforts have demanded large sacrifices in the Latin American population's standard of living, which in some cases is reaching extreme limits. . . .

G. They reiterated that each country is responsible for the negotiation of its own external debt. Likewise, they warned that recent experiences prove that the problem of the developing countries' external debts cannot be resolved solely through a dialogue with the banks, the isolated action of multilateral financial organizations, or regular market activities. Therefore, the definition and acceptance of general reorganization and financing guidelines or policies, which serve as a reference framework for each country's individual negotiations, is deemed necessary.

H. They agreed that this reference framework must bear in mind the joint responsibilities of the parties involved in the search for a permanent solution to the problem.

I. They also agreed that this framework must ensure an equitable distribution of the economic reorganization's costs. . . .

J. They stressed that there is a close relationship among the debt problems, financings, and trade to strengthen the regional countries' ability to pay by stimulating economic growth through an increase in exports, the resuming of financial flow, and maintaining adequate levels in the ability to export.

K. In addition, they pointed out the urgent need for the industrial countries to adopt measures and policies to facilitate the access of developing countries' exports to their markets. They also indicated the urgent need for the industrial countries to create conditions that allow for the resuming of financial flow and a continued and significant alleviation of debt interests, without which the Latin American countries' efforts toward an economic reorganization would be null and void.

L. The foreign and finance ministers said that direct foreign investment can play a complementary role because of its capital contribution and technology transfer, the jobs created, and the exports generated, provided this investment abides by the area countries' policies and legislation on the matter. However, the contribution of this direct foreign investment—in terms of foreign exchange—to the solution of the international imbalance is limited; and for this reason it could not constitute a determining factor in the solution of the foreign debt problems.

M. The foreign and finance ministers received well the Colombian president's urging to create an international financing system that allows for the vigorous growth of developing countries in order for them to raise their peoples' standard of living. Among others, the fundamental ideas that have served as a basis for this consensus should be taken into consideration for such a system.

N. They determined to urge the industrial countries' governments and international banks to give proper attention to the proposals presented in the Consensus of Cartagena to find a stable, in-depth solution to the problems of Latin America's foreign debt.

Proposals

O. Based on what was discussed in this consensus, the foreign ministers and ministers in charge of the financial sectors decided to propose the following:

1. The adoption of measures that lead to a sharp and immediate reduction of the nominal and real interest rates in international markets
2. That international banks use reference rates that in no case surpass the real costs of revenues in the market . . .
3. The reduction to a minimum of operations costs and other expenses, as well as the elimination of commissions, and the abolition of interest for delayed payments during renegotiation periods
4. The use of temporary mechanisms to soften the impact of high interest rates, such as a compensatory financing facility of the IMF
5. The renegotiation operations should take into account the characteristics of the debt and each country's economic recovery capacity and payment ability. Terms and grace periods must be substantially improved
6. That in the case of countries with extreme balance of payments problems, clauses considered to permit the postponement of payment of parts of the interests that—without incurring additional interests—would be paid with a specific proportion of revenues stemming from an increase of exports
7. That the renegotiation of external debts should not compromise export revenues beyond reasonable percentages . . .
8. Elimination of the regulatory rigidities of some international financial centers that automatically punish the credit portfolios of developing countries and prevent the granting of new financing, and recognition of the special quality that the sovereign countries have as debtors in the international financial community and adapting the existing regulations to that quality
9. Reactivation of the credit flow toward the debtor countries that in many cases has been virtually suspended . . .

10. The allocation of a larger volume of resources and strengthening of the credit capacity of the international financial organizations such as the IMF, the World Bank, and the IDB

11. A new allocation of special drawing rights in the IMF compatible with the liquid needs of the developing countries, an increase of the time limits of their adjustment programs, and an expansion of the access to their resources

12. Revision of the criteria used by the IMF to give priority to the increase of production and employment . . .

13. The utilization of World Bank and IDB resources should be accelerated and increased . . .

14. Debtor countries should be granted much longer terms and even more preferential interest rates in the renegotiation of their debts with governments and official credit organizations to exports from the industrial countries

15. Immediate attention should be given to the demands of developing countries regarding the stabilization of their products' prices at profitable levels . . .

16. The rapid elimination of tariff and nontariff barriers of industrial countries that limit the access of developing countries' products to their markets, both for traditional products and industrial products, including high technology.

P. In order to carry out the outlines and proposals expressed in this consensus, advocate a dialogue with creditor countries, keep the international economic situation constantly under surveillance, and evaluate the enforcement of the proposed initiatives, the foreign and finance ministers determined to maintain a regional consultation and follow-up mechanism. This mechanism will be open to the participation of the other countries of the region.

Q. They stated that the need for this dialogue is expressed in the contents of the 5 June letter to the participants of the London summit, in which it was stressed that "it is urgent that the international community tackle in a comprehensive and coherent manner the problems of the world's economy, recognizing the interrelations that tie them together, and find satisfactory solutions in an interdependent world."

R. They agreed to fully use existing forums to discuss and analyze the foreign debt, particularly at the Development Committee of the International Bank for Reconstruction and Development (IBRD), in which they will propose the establishment of a "working group" for this matter.

S. They expressed their willingness to hold a meeting with governments of industrialized countries for a joint reflection on the multiple aspects and the economic, social, and political consequences of the Latin American foreign debt, bearing in mind the need to find a solution to the excessive burden it represents and to create favorable conditions for reactivating the development of indebted countries and a sustained expansion of the world's economy and trade, safeguarding the interests of all the parties involved.

Mar del Plata Communiqué, September 13-14, 1984

A. They expressed concern over the fact that while poverty intensifies in the developing countries, the industrialized countries are losing their sense of urgency with respect to finding a solution to the foreign debt crisis. They stated that although the international financial system has not yet become severely destabilized, the impact of the crisis is being felt more deeply in their countries.

In light of these facts, which must be handled within a broad political context, the Ministers agreed:

1. To ratify the Consensus of Cartagena
2. To reiterate their solidarity with regard to the Latin American debt problem
3. To reaffirm their determination to continue to consult with one another, as often as necessary, within the framework of the consultation and follow-up mechanism

B. They noted that the rise in interest rates that occurred soon after the conclusion of the Cartagena meeting aggravated the negative consequences caused by the already excessively high level of such rates. This confirms the urgent need for the international community, and especially the governments of the industrialized countries, to take actions designed to restore real interest rates to reasonable levels.

C. They reiterated their concern that adjustment efforts made by one side still have not been matched by the other. This is not compatible with the idea of creditors and debtors sharing responsibility in the search for a solution to the debt problem.

D. They reaffirmed the need for dialogue as a factor in reaching an understanding.

Meeting in Santo Domingo, February 7-8, 1985

A. New Considerations

1. Debt restructurings are not sufficient and merely postpone the problem
2. The persistent application of stringent adjustment programs has continued to entail, in general, a drastic reduction of the material levels of living and well-being of the broad mass of the Latin American population
3. Social tensions have reached critical levels, owing to the scope and rapidity of the adjustment processes applied
4. The transfer of financial resources became negative for the region, amounting to an estimated $55,000 million in the past two years.

B. Political Dialogue

1. The Ministers consider it essential to reiterate firmly their belief that there can be no stable and permanent solution to the external debt problem unless the Governments of debtor and creditor countries agree on an appropriate political framework for these questions as a whole
2. In accordance with the foregoing, the Ministers decided on the following course of action:
   a. To present to the forthcoming meetings of the Interim Committee of the International Monetary Fund (IMF) and the World Bank-IMF Development Committee, on 17 and 18 April 1985, a *joint position* based on the agreement reached in Santo Domingo.
   b. To make a joint approach to the industrialized countries participating in the forthcoming Bonn meeting, placing before them proposals for dealing with the external debt problem in its various aspects;
   c. To draw the attention of international public opinion to the magnitude of the problem and to the serious consequences that might ensue if it is not dealt with in an appropriate political framework.

Meeting in Montevideo, December 16-17, 1985

A. In the last five years the standard of living of the Latin American countries has regressed a decade. The most severe adjustment can not compensate for the very *heavy weight of the debt service derived in great part from high interest rates.* . . .

B. The absence of growth generates grave problems which open the door to instability and social tensions and endanger the consolidation of democratic processes. Here is what 1985 has left us:

1. *A new fall in income per inhabitant.* A large negative transfer of real resources toward the exterior
2. The net transfer was about $30 billion, more than in 1984, totaling more than $100 billion in the last four years
3. Various external factors, especially the *dramatic fall of prices,* have caused a new fall in the value of exports of the region estimated at $6 billion this year
4. *The level of investment is a third less than in the year 1980.* These numbers teach a lesson. The international economy is experiencing a stage of profound economic disequilibriums of a global character that affect all aspects of the international economy. Therefore the crisis ought to be addressed in an integrated form, if one wants to avoid even greater disequilibriums. So, it's indispensable to *reaffirm the objective of growth and, for that, there is required the urgent adoption of a group of emergency measures while developed countries realize the structural adjustments that will permit normalization of international conditions, with the aim of recovering a dynamic and sustained development.*

C. *The Baker Proposal represents a positive step in recognizing the principle of coresponsibility in the solution of the debt problem and the necessity of growth by the debtor countries through the reestablishment of financial flows to those countries.* Nevertheless, the proposal is insufficient in that the debt problem in not limited to the need for a flow of funds, given that the volume of resources envisaged would only with difficulty reach the amount which would permit the debtor countries to meet their obligations to their creditors and at the same time assure their own sustained growth. Further, there are important questions about the proposal to clarify participation by the debtor countries in this effort would be useful. The proposal also fails to specify the implications of the conditionality which it implies on the part of the IMF agreements and the structural adjustment programs of the World Bank. It does not contemplate the situation of various debtor countries that need fresh funds immediately and amounts difficult to reconcile with the amounts envisaged in the proposal. The Baker Proposal does not include Latin American and Caribbean debtor countries, such as the Dominican Republic, which will not have access to additional external financing. In this sense, the Cartagena consensus countries express their solidarity with the debt problem of the relatively less developed countries.

D. The permanent solution to the debt problem will be achieved when the *developed country governments assume their responsibilities to reduce their structural rigidities, assure a sustained growth in the international economy, and achieve a structural equilibrium.* This goal requires time, but *Latin America can't wait.* It is necessary to implement quickly a package of emergency measures.

E. The growth of the Latin American economies is a requirement that cannot be postponed, and to which ought to be subordinated the schemes for the solution of the debt problem.

F. As a goal it is proposed that *the region's gross national product double by the end of the century.* Outward resource flows ought to be reversed to assure a *level of investments compatible with the attainment of that goal.* Further, only adequate investment will allow the countries to become part of the process of technological change which, on improving the competitiveness of their economies, will allow them to achieve their trade balance goals. But, current *protectionist measures by industrial countries could frustrate both investments and technological progress.*

G. This emergency proposal of Montevideo for the negotiation of the debt and for growth is of a temporary nature and contains the following measures:

1. Return of *real interest rates* to historical levels and *reduction of high interest*
2. *Increase the flow of funds and separate the current debt from new debt*
3. *Maintenance of the real balances of credit from the commercial banks.* That is, *the annual increase in bank credits should at least be equal to the rate of inflation.*
4. Limit on the net transfer of resources. It is necessary to establish a maximum for *outward transfer linked to a minimum growth goal for GNP.* There

could also be established *limits on debt service* in relation to export income which would be compatible with the needs of development and the social and economic requirements of each country.

Some countries of the *group recognize the negative effect of capital flight and their responsibility regarding that phenomenon.* At the same time, they recognize the attitude of stimulating these capital movements which can frequently be observed in the creditor countries.

5. Substantial *increase in the resources of the multilateral development institutions. A net annual increase of 20 percent for the next three years is proposed.... Existing conditionality should be revised to make it compatible with the growth targets, and additional conditionality associated with the increased resources, which might become an obstacle to the use of the resources, ought to be avoided.*

6. Paris Club.

   Industrial country governments ought to provide for the countries that need them *multiyear restructurings of principal and the capitalization of interest without suspending cover for new export credits as a result of the restructuring and without demanding the existence of a formal accord between the debtor country and the IMF.*

7. IMF.

   The IMF should *expand its compensatory financing facility* so as to permit financing of not only the impact on the balance of payments of falling export earnings, but also the impacts of other external factors such as deterioration in the terms of trade, continuing high interest rates, and natural disasters.

   Amounts available through this facility should be expanded appropriately with very *low conditionality and medium terms.*

8. Conditionality.

   The conditionality of the IMF ought to take into the account the *requirements for growth and production and employment, just as it ought to respect the capability of each country to formulate and execute its plans of adjustment.*

9. International Trade.

   The success of all actions undertaken with respect to the debt will depend in the medium and long term on the capacity of the debtor countries to increase substantially their export incomes. Therefore, it is indispensable that *protectionist measures cease.*

If the package of proposed measures should not be adopted, the region would see itself in a situation of extreme gravity which would oblige it necessarily to limit its net transfers of resources to avoid a greater social and political instability which could reverse the processes of democratic consolidation.

Notwithstanding the fact that since the formation of the Cartagena consensus in June of 1984 the difficulties and the economic crisis have maintained themselves as we have explained, *the exercise of solidarity among our nations has permitted us to advance toward some of the objectives which we proposed.* The disregard of the creditor country governments of the debt problem of the region *has been replaced by their recognition of their coresponsibility and by the political dialogue which, as a result, has been initiated.*

Meeting in Punta del Este, February 28, 1986

A. During the meeting, an analysis was made of the impact of the sudden drop in the price of petroleum on the economies of certain countries of region which are important petroleum exporters. A high degree of Latin American solidarity was reaffirmed, as well as the necessity for certain countries to take concrete measures in defense of their economies, in the area of debt.

B. The committee concluded that in the case of certain countries, despite notable efforts which have been taken at internal adjustment, *the point has been reached at which significant modifications in existing agreements can no longer be delayed, particularly with regard to interest rates,* in order that creditors and debtors share more equitably the burden of adjustment.

C. These and other emergency actions, which may be taken in accordance with the situation in each country and in the exercise of its proper sovereignty, will have the full support of the member countries of the Cartagena consensus.

D. It was decided to maintain close contact among the members of the consensus in order to follow the evolution of those economies most affected during the coming weeks, as well as the progress which can be achieved in formulating solutions to lessen the impact of the fall in export earnings.

Selected Bibliography

Books

Agency for International Development, Department of State. *A Study on Loan Terms, Debt Burden and Development*. Washington, D.C., April 1965.

Balassa, Bela, Gerardo M. Bueno, Pedro-Pablo Kuczynski, and Mario Henrique Simonsen. *Toward Renewed Economic Growth in Latin America*. Washington, D.C.: Institute for International Economics, 1986.

Bergsten, C. Fred, William R. Cline, and John Williamson. *Bank Lending to Developing Countries: The Policy Alternatives*. Washington, D.C.: Institute for International Economics, 1985.

Bernstein, Marvin D. *Foreign Investment in Latin America: Cases and Attitudes*. New York: Alfred Knopf, 1966.

Cline, William R. *International Debt: Systemic Risk and Policy Response*. Washington, D.C.: Institute for International Economics, 1984.

Commonwealth Secretariat. *The Debt Crisis and the World Economy*. London: Marlborough House, 1984.

Enders, Thomas O., and Richard P. Mattione. *Latin America: The Crisis of Debt and Growth*. Washington, D.C.: The Brookings Institution, 1985.

Feinberg, Richard E., and Valeriana Kallab (eds.). *Adjustment Crisis in the Third World*. New Brunswick, N.J.: Transaction Books for Overseas Development Council, 1984.

———*Uncertain Future: Commercial Banks and the Third World*. New Brunswick, N.J.: Transaction Books for Overseas Development Council, 1984.

Frank, Charles et al. *Assisting Developing Countries: Problems of Debts, Burden-Sharing, Jobs and Trade*. New York: Praeger, 1972.

Green, Rosario. *El endeudamiento publico externo de México*. México: El Colegio de México, 1976.

Inter-American Development Bank. *External Debt and Economic Development in Latin America: Background and Prospects*. Washington, D.C.: IDB, 1984.

Inter-American Dialogue. *Rebuilding Cooperation in the Americas*. Washington, D.C.: Aspen Institute, April 1986.

Lessard, Donald R., and John Williamson. *Financial Intermediation Beyond the Debt Crisis*. Washington, D.C.: Institute for International Economics, 1985.

Lipson, Charles. *Standing Guard: Protecting Foreign Capital in the Nineteenth and Twentieth Centuries*. Berkeley: University of California Press, 1985.

Mamalakis, Markos J. (ed.). *Inter-American Economic Relations: The New Development View,* special issue of *Journal of Interamerican Studies and World Affairs* 27, no. 4 (Winter 1985-86).

Moran, Theodore H. *Investing in Development: New Roles for Private Capital?* New Brunswick, N.J.: Transaction Books for the Overseas Development Council, 1986.

Pastor, Robert A. *Congress and the Politics of U.S. Foreign Economic Policy.* Berkeley: University of California Press, 1980.

———*U.S. Foreign Investment in Latin America: The Impact on Employment.* Buenos Aires: Institute for Latin American Integration of the Inter-American Development Bank, 1984.

Payer, Cheryl. *The Debt Trap: The International Monetary Fund and the Third World.* New York and London: Monthly Review Press, 1974.

Watkins, Alfred J. *Till Debt Do Us Part: Who Wins, Who Loses, and Who Pays For the International Debt Crisis.* Lanham, N.Y. and London: University Press of America, 1986.

Williamson, John. *The Lending Policies of the Internatioal Monetary Fund.* Washington, D.C.: Institute for International Economics, 1982.

Wionczek, Miguel S. *LDC External Debt and the World Economy.* México: El Colegio de México and Center for Economic and Social Studies of the Third World, 1978.

Articles

Avramovic, Dragoslav. "Debts in Early 1985: An Institutional Impasse." *Journal of Development Planning* 16 (1985): pp. 105-121.

Blejer, Mario I., and Mohsim S. Khan. "Private Investment in Developing Countries." *Finance and Development* 21, no. 2 (June 1984): pp. 26-29.

Bogdanowicz-Bindert, Christine A. "World Debt; The United States Reconsiders." *Foreign Affairs* (Winter 1985-86).

Brainard, Lawrence. "More Lending to the Third World? A Banker's View." In Feinberg, Richard E., and Valeriana Kallab (eds.). *Uncertain Future: Commercial Banks and the Third World.* New Brunswick, N.J.: Transaction Books for Overseas Development Council, 1984.

Cline, William R. "Debt, Macro Policy and State Intervention: The Next Phase for Latin America." *Journal of Inter-American Studies and World Affairs* 27, no. 4 (Winter 1985-86): pp. 155-172.

Diaz-Alejandro, Carlos. "Latin American Debt: I Don't Think We Are In Kansas Anymore." *Brookings Papers on Economic Activity* 2 (1984): pp. 335-403.

Ffrench-Davis, Ricardo. "International Private Lending and Borrowing Strategies of Developing Countries." *Journal of Development Planning* 14 (1984): pp. 119-164.

Fishlow, Albert. "The Debt Crisis: Round Two Ahead?" In Feinberg, Richard E., and Valeriana Kallab (eds.). *Adjustment Crisis in the Third World.* New Brunswick, N.J.: Transaction Books for Overseas Development Council, 1984.

Fletcher, Richard D. "Lessons of Recent Debt Reorganization." In Haq, Khadija (ed.). *The Lingering Debt Crisis.* Islamabad: North-South Roundtable, 1985.

Hector, Gary. "Third World Debt: The Bomb Is Defused." *Fortune* 18 (February 1985): pp. 36-50.

Kissinger, Henry A. "Building a Bridge of Hope to Our Latin Neighbors." *Washington Post,* June 25, 1985, p. 15A.

Kuczynski, Pedro-Pablo. "Latin American Debt: Act Two." *Foreign Affairs* (Fall 1983): pp. 17-38.

Lever, Harold. "The Debt Won't Be Paid." *The New York Review of Books,* June 28, 1984, pp. 3-5.

Massad, Carlos. "Debt: An Overview." *Journal of Development Planning* 16 (1985): pp. 3-21.

Ohlin, Goran. "Debts, Developments and Default." In Helleiner, G.K. (ed.). *A World Divided: The Less Developed Countries in the International Economy.* London, New York, and Melbourne: Cambridge University Press, 1976, pp. 207-224.

Orlando, Frank, and Simon Teitel, "Latin America's External Debt Problem: Debt-Servicing Strategies." In Edwards, Sebastian, and Simon Teitel (eds.). *Growth, Reform, and Adjustment: Latin America's Trade and Macroeconomic Policies in the 1970s and 1980s,* a special issue of *Economic Development and Cultural Change* 34, no. 3 (April 1986).

Pfeffermann, Guy P. "World Bank Policies in Relation to the External Debt of Member Countries." In Mehran, H. (ed.). *External Debt Management.* Washington, D.C.: IMF, 1985.

"President García Delivers Inaugural Address." *Foreign Broadcast Information Services,* July 29, 1985, pp. J3-J24.

Roett, Riordan. "Democracy and Debt in South America: A Continent's Dilemma." *Foreign Affairs, America and the World 1983,* pp. 695-720.

Saxe, Jo W. "The External Debt of Developing Countries." *The External Banker's Association for Foreign Trade* (May 1977): pp. 1-19.

Solomon, Robert. "A Perspective on the Debt of Developing Countries." *Brookings Papers on Economic Activity* 2 (1972): pp. 479-510.

"The LDC Debt Problem—at the Midpoint?" *World Financial Markets* (October-November 1984): pp. 1-19.

Van Agtmael, W. Antoine. "Evaluating the Risks of Lending to Developing Countries." *Euromoney* (April 1976): pp. 16-30.

Weinert, Richard S. "Swapping Third World Debt." *Foreign Policy* 65 (Winter 1986-87): pp. 85-97

Documents

Latin American Economic System

"Renegotiation of Latin America's External Debt: Proposals for the Implementation of the Quito Declaration and Plan of Action." Caracas, March 1984

United Nations

"Debt Problems of Developing Countries, External Payments and Receipts by Developing Countries Associated with Official and Private Capital Transactions." Note by the UNCTAD Secretariat. Geneva, December 11, 1974.

"Multilateral Debt Renegotiations—Experience of Fund Members." Study prepared by the staff of the International Monetary Fund. Note by the UNCTAD Secretariat, Trade and Development Board. Geneva, December 11, 1974.

"Problems of Debt Servicing." Paper by the IBRD on Rescheduling or Consolidation of External Debt. Note by the UNCTAD Secretariat, Trade and Development Board. New York, April 4, 1967.

"The Economic Crisis: Policies for Adjustment, Stabilization, and Growth." Paper prepared for the Economic Commission for Latin America and the Caribbean. Mexico City, April 8, 1986.

"The Problem of the External Debt: Gestation, Development, Crisis, and Prospects." Paper prepared for the Economic Commission for Latin America and the Caribbean. Mexico City, March 6, 1986.

U.S. Congress

Joint Economic Committee. *The Impact of the Latin American Debt Crisis on the U.S. Economy.* Washington, D.C., May 10, 1986.

Contributors

Manuel Azpúrua has been the minister of finance of Venezuela since February 1984. He holds a law degree from the Central University of Venezuela and is a partner in the law firm of Mendoza, Palacios, Acedo, Borgas, Páez, and Pumar. As finance minister, he has been chiefly responsible for Venezuela's debt negotiations.

Howard Baker is currently White House chief of staff. Prior to his appointment by President Ronald Reagan in March 1987, he was a senior partner in the Washington law firm of Vinson and Elkins. He was senator from Tennessee from 1966 to 1985, serving as Republican Senate majority leader from 1981 to 1985. As senator, he served on several committees, including Foreign Relations. He was a candidate for the Republican presidential nomination in 1980.

C. Fred Bergsten is currently director of the Institute for International Economics. From 1977 to 1981 he served as assistant secretary of the Treasury for international affairs. He has been a senior fellow at the Carnegie Endowment for International Peace (1981) and at the Brookings Institution (1972–1976). From 1969 to 1971 he served as advisor for international economic affairs on the National Security Council. Dr. Bergsten is the author of fifteen books and numerous articles on international economic issues, including *Bank Lending to Developing Countries: The Policy Alternatives*.

Bill Bradley was elected to the U.S. Senate from New Jersey in 1978. His assignments have included membership in the Finance Committee, the Energy Committee, and the Select Committee on Intelligence. An honors graduate of Princeton University and a Rhodes Scholar at Oxford, Senator Bradley is the author of *Life on the Run*, a book dealing with his experiences as an athlete, and *The Fair Tax*, an explanation of his proposal to revise the income tax system.

Terence C. Canavan is executive vice president and head of the Latin America and Southeast Asia divisions of the World Banking Group of Chemical Bank. Mr. Canavan was Chemical Bank's representative in Caracas from

1964 to 1968, in Mexico City from 1969 to 1970, and in Madrid from 1971 to 1972. Previously, he was a senior vice president (1979) and headed the Latin American region offices in the International Division.

Jimmy Carter was the thirty-ninth president of the United States and Georgia's seventy-sixth governor. Since leaving Washington, President Carter has written three books: *Keeping Faith: Memoirs of a President* (1982), *The Blood of Abraham* (1985), and *Everything to Gain: Making the Most of the Rest of Your Life* (with Rosalynn Carter, 1987). In April 1982, he accepted appointment as Emory University distinguished professor, and in September of that year, the Carter Center of Emory University was established.

Richard E. Feinberg is vice president of the Overseas Development Council. Before joining the council in 1981, he served as the Latin American specialist on the policy planning staff of the U.S. Department of State and as an international economist in the Treasury Department and with the House Banking Committee. Dr. Feinberg is the author of numerous articles and books on international economic and political issues, including *The Intemperate Zone: The Third World Challenge to U.S. Foreign Policy.*

Albert Fishlow is currently chairman of the Economics Department at the University of California, Berkeley. From 1978 to 1983 he was professor of economics and chairman of the Center for International and Area Studies at Yale University. From 1975 to 1976 he was deputy assistant secretary of state for inter-American affairs. Dr. Fishlow is on the editorial boards of *Foreign Policy* and *International Organization.* He is the author of many books and articles on economic development, the economy of Brazil, and North-South economic relations.

Pedro-Pablo Kuczynski is co-chairman of the First Boston International Company and has been managing director of First Boston Corporation since 1982. Kuczynski was minister of mines and energy in Peru from 1980 to 1982. He received a B.A. from Exeter College, Oxford, and an M.P.A. from Princeton University as a John Parker Compton Fellow. He is the author of *Peruvian Democracy Under Economic Stress: An Account of the Belaunde Administration, 1963-68.*

David C. Mulford has served as assistant secretary of the treasury since January 1984. Prior to entering public service, he was senior investment advisor for the Saudi Arabia Monetary Agency (1974-1984). Mulford received his Ph.D. from St. Anthony's College, Oxford University, in 1965.

Daniel Oduber is president of the Policy Committee of the National Liberation party (PLN) of Costa Rica and vice president of the Socialist International. He was president of Costa Rica from 1974 to 1978. Before that, he served as president of the Legislative Assembly and minister of foreign relations. President Oduber began his political career in 1945 as a founder of the Social Democratic party of Costa Rica. In addition, he has authored numerous books and articles on Costa Rica and on the PLN.

Robert A. Pastor is director of the Latin American and Caribbean program of the Carter Center and professor of political science at Emory University. He served as the director of Latin American and Caribbean Affairs on the National Security Council of the White House (1977-1981). Dr. Pastor received his Ph.D. from Harvard University and is the author of numerous articles and books, including *Condemned to Repetition: The United States and Nicaragua, Migration and Development in the Caribbean: The Unexplored Connection,* and *Congress and the Politics of U.S. Foreign Economic Policy: 1929-1976.*

William R. Rhodes is chairman of Citibank's Restructuring Committee. He joined Citibank in 1957 and served in many foreign posts. In 1975, he became senior vice president in charge of the Andean and Caribbean regions. Mr. Rhodes is a trustee and member of the executive council of the Council of the Americas, a director of the Americas' Society, and a member of the Council on Foreign Relations.

Jésus Silva-Herzog was Mexico's minister of finance and public credit from 1982 to 1986. He was under-secretary of finance from 1979 to 1982. In addition, he served as director of the Office of Technical Assistance of the Bank of Mexico, director general of public credit of the Secretariat of Finance and Public Credit, and director of the Institute of the National Fund for Worker's Housing. He is the author of books and articles on economic development.

J. Gustave Speth is president of the World Resources Institute, a center for policy research and environmental issues, and professor of law at Georgetown University Law Center. Mr. Speth was the chair of the Council on Environmental Quality in the Executive Office of the President (1977–1981) and co-chair of the President's Task Force on Global Resources and Environment.

Eduardo Wiesner has served as director of the Western Hemisphere Department for the International Monetary Fund since 1982. He was Colombia's minister of planning (1978) and minister of finance (1980). Mr. Wiesner holds a master's degree in economics from Stanford University and has written extensively about economic development, public finance, and the debt crisis.

Index